Mu1 Muneeb-ur

Grand Mufti of Pakistan

THE REFORMATION OF BELIEFS AND PRACTICES OF AHL AS-SUNNAH WAL-JAMAAH

Translated by
Dr Musharraf Hussain Al-Azhari, OBE, DL

Published by Jama'at-e-Ahl as-Sunnah (UK)
Invitation Publishing

The reformation of the beliefs and practices of Ahl As-Sunnah Wal-Jamaah
By Mufti Muneeb-ur-Rehman

Translated into English by Dr Musharraf Hussain

First edition published March 2021

INVITATION PUBLISHING LTD
512-514 Berridge Road West
Nottingham
NG7 5JU

Tel: +44[0] 115 8550961
E-mail: info@invitationpublishing.co.uk
https://www.invitationpublishing.co.uk

Distributed by INVITATION PUBLISHING LTD.

ISBN: 9781902248899

Cataloguing-in-Publication Data is available from the British Library.

Dedication

"To the bold scholars and spiritual guides, the Pirs of Ahl As-Sunnah Wal -Jamaah who stood up with me against the charlatans and deviant innovators. They are my fellow travellers. May Allah protect them, give them health and well-being; may he grant them steadfastness so they may be light for the society now and the future generations".

Acknowledgement

I acknowledge the support given by Mufti Muhammad Ilyas Ashrafi Rizvi and Mufti Waseem Akhtar al-Madani. They read the manuscript several times and revised it thoroughly and I am grateful to other scholars who provided advice to make this book authentic.

Prophet Shoaib proclaimed boldly, *"I wish to reform society to the best of my ability. My success depends entirely on Allah, I put my trust in Him and I turn in repentance to Him"* (Hud: 88).

The beloved Messenger ﷺ said, "religion is sincerity" the disciples asked, "sincerity to who?" He replied, "sincerity to Allah, to his book, to his Messenger, to the Muslim leaders and the public" (Muslim).

Muhammad Ibn Sireen said, "this knowledge is the religion, so be careful from who you learn religion" (Muslim).

Foreword

Allah, the Lord of the worlds is the praiseworthy. Blessings on the beloved Messenger Muhammad ﷺ, his family and all the disciples.

Scholars and spiritual guides, the Pirs who are passionate about Islam and their school of thought have shown concern about some errors and poor practices that have crept into the Ahl As-Sunnah Wal-Jamaah over the years. They have reflected on how to reform them and which strategy to adopt. Some of these practices have become a means of livelihood for some people. When they are criticised, they turn to blackmailing and bullying. In such a tense environment most people prefer the dispensation to remain silent for the sake of safety and honour. They avoid challenging them. But we believe Islam is our identity and our honour. We must do everything and be determined to safeguard the honour of Islam.

After consultation with scholars and the spiritual guides of Ahl As-sunnah Wal-Jamaah, I decided to write this book. I saw it my duty to point out the bad practices and to reform them. I called it 'the reformation of beliefs and practices.' I want to reform and correct the deviant. This is not to humiliate anyone nor to target any individual or an organisation. I believe Ahl As-Sunnah Wal-Jamaah is one community, one body and this is an effort to self-reform and self-development. I don't claim this document is the final word on reformation, rather it is a small step and an earnest attempt to reform. Therefore, others are invited to improve and add to it. So regard this as a foundation to build on.

I invited the finest trustworthy Muftis of Karachi to be my partners and by the grace of Allah, they responded positively without the slightest hesitation. Mufti Muhammad Waseem and I wrote the first draft of the book. This was revised by Mufti Muhammad Ilyas Akhtar, Mufti Muhammad Akmal Madani, Mufti M Ismael Nurani.

THE REFORMATION OF BELIEFS AND PRACTICES OF AHL AS-SUNNAH WAL-JAMA'AH

Contents

What senior scholars say about this book

Pir Syed Haseen-udeen Shah
(Founder of Zia ul uloom, Rawalpindi, Pakistan)
After consultation with the scholars and the spiritual guides of Ahl As-Suunah Wal-Jamaah mufti Muneeb-ur-Rehman has compiled this book. It has been supported and endorsed by many people… Purpose is not to target any individual or organisation but Reformation, therefore, all the scholars must read this book with open mind and acknowledge the compilers good intention and accept his endeavours according to the prophetic saying "religion is a sincere reminder."… I request scholars to spread the message of the book and cooperate in delivering it to others.

Allama Faiza-ur-Rasul Rizvi
(Jamia Muhadis Azam, Faisalabad, Pakistan)
Today Ah As-Sunnah Wal-Jamaah is passing through a painful crisis, it's not a secret. Innovations in beliefs and practices have disenfranchised the religious community. To reform these innovations Mufti Muneeb-ur-Rehman has masterly composed this book. It's a unique contribution. May Allah reward Mufti Sahib abundantly through his beloved Messenger ﷺ.

Allama Ghulam Rabbani Afghani
(Founder of Faizan-e-Islam, London, UK)
Friends and adversaries acknowledge the scholarship, the communication skills and managerial capabilities of Mufti Muneeb-ur-Rehman. Through 'the reformation of beliefs and practices' he has rendered an amazing service to Ahl As-Sunnah Wal-Jamaah. This is a witness to his boldness and passion for the Ummah. I studied it from beginning to the end. The method of presenting evidence is effective and impressive. May Allah accept this sincere endeavour.

Pir Habeeb-ur Rehman Mahboobi
(Founder of Jamia Suffat-ul Islam, Bradford, UK)

The compiler Mufti Muneeb-ur-Rehman unreservedly wants the reformation of Ahl As-Sunnah Wal-Jamaah, therefore according to the prophetic saying "the value of deeds depends on the intention". I pray, Allah reward him abundantly. I believe Mufti Muneeb-ur-Rehman is 'the proof of Islam', a man of authority. This book will help to rectify many misconceptions about Ala-Hazrat. This book accurately represents the teachings of the Quran and Sunnah. The author has authoritatively proven that Ala-Hazrat was not a founder of the new thought or a sect but a representative of the authentic Ahl As-Sunnah Wal-Jamaah. He was the commentator of the Quran and the Sunnah and Hanafi jurisprudence. I request all scholars, Mashaikh to adopt this as a text for their students and disciples.

Allama Dr Noor-ul-Haq Qadri
(Federal Minister of Religious Affairs, Government of Pakistan)

This book is a brave and bold attempt by Mufti Muneeb-ur-Rehman to reform Ahl As-Sunnah Wal-Jamaah, may Allah grant him reward.

Allama Muhammad Rafiq Hassani
(Principal of Jamia Islamia, Karachi, Pakistan)

I fully endorse and approve everything Mufti Muneeb-ur-Rehman has written in this book. It was direly needed, a strong assertive voice was needed, since the situation has got so bad. In such circumstances reform can only be done through reprimand and firmness… I pray for the mufti's success.

Pir Khwaja Muhammad Hassan Barawi
(Fateh Pur, Liya, Pakistan)

Thinker of Islam Mufti Muneeb-ur-Rehman is a competent jurist of our time, a true spokesperson of Ahl As-Sunnah Wal-Jamaah. Unfortunately, the opponents of the Jamaah have been attacking it and branding it as Barelvi sect. Yet Ala-Hazrat was the Imam and reformer of 20th-century. He was called Barelvi because he came from the city of Bareilly in India.

Mufti Muneeb-ur-Rehman has used the power of his pen to reform the beliefs and practices of Ahl As-Sunnah Wal-Jamaah. This is a great gift for us all.

Allama Muhammad Naseerullah Naqashbandi
(Imam of Jamia Madinah Mosque, Bolton, UK)

Mufti Muneeb-ur-Rehman has not only identified the innovations and bad practices in the religious gatherings but presented ways of reforming them. He has given evidence from authentic scholarly sources. I hope scholars, Mashaikh and preachers will appreciate this endeavour and will play their part in this reformative movement…. This book will remain as a beacon of light for a long time according to this verse *"that which is useful becomes established in the world"* (Al-Raad: 17). Mufti Muneeb-ur-Rehman is the pride of Ahl As-Sunnah Wal-Jamaah, may Allah protect him.

Allama Ansar ul Qadri
(Jamiat Tabligh al Islam, Bradford, UK)

I believe this book will be beneficial for everyone whether a scholar, shaykh, teacher, preacher or student. This discourse will be a beacon in our time of ignorance it will guide the misguided and be a source of inspiration. Mufti Muneeb-ur-Rehman has played a role of super leader, in him I see a likeness of the venerable teachers of the past. His writing style is effective, he does not sprinkle salt over wounds but puts bandages to sooth them. He doesn't shout and blame but presents well-argued discourse that is impressive.

Professor Dr Zafar Iqbal Jalali
(Principal of Jamia Islamabad, Pakistan)

Mufti Muneeb-ur-Rehman is our beloved and popular scholar, he has many amazing qualities, clear thinking, intelligence, gentleness, piety and magnanimity. When I received 'The Reformation of Beliefs and practices' I was over the moon. The disease was diagnosed correctly and the arguments presented solidly from authentic sources. This endeavour fills the need of our time.

Allama Muhammad Mazhar Fareed Shah
(Jamia Fareedia, Siyawal, Pakistan)

Justice and the middle way are the principles on which the world functions, it is the antithesis of extremism. These beliefs, practices and moral values will only be fruitful when they are done in a moderate way. The separation of healthy from the sick, the real from the fake, acceptable from the rejected and truth from falsehood is paramount for any movement to revive religion. So, we ask Allah to accept the beautiful endeavours of Mufti Muneeb-ur-Rehman.

Allama Manzar-ul Islam
(Islamic centre, North Carolina, USA)

Ahl As-Sunnah Wal-Jamaah (Bralilvi group) is badly broken and disunited, it seems it has no central authority. In this time of crisis Mufti Muneeb-ur-Rehman has stood up and played the role of a smart leader. This was his calling, when others were silent, he stood up and boldly challenged the deviant people. May Allah bless his efforts.

Translator's introduction

Mufti Muneeb-ur-Rehman; A man of integrity, piety and scholarship. A tribute to the Grand Mufti of Pakistan

Mufti Muneeb-ur-Rehman has turned 75 years young and retired from the National Moonsighting Committee. He is best known as the chairman of the moon sighting committee of Pakistan. Over the past 20 years he has been a household name in the country; thrice a year he heralded the onset of the holy month of Ramadan or the joy of Eid. He is the embodiment of humility and gentleness, a representative of time-honoured pious teachers of the past and a passionate defender of Islamic values and modesty. His reputation as a champion of Islam and the Patriotic Pakistani precedes him wherever he travels. He is unarguably one of the most prominent scholars of Pakistan.

He holds or has formerly held several high national offices: the President of Tanzeem-ul-Madaris Pakistan, the nation's largest association of religious schools numbering more than 30,000 with two million students; member of the Islamic Ideology; Professor at Jinnah University for Women; Member of The National Academic Council of Institute of Policy Studies; Head of Shariah Board of Burj Bank and President of Darul Uloom Naeemia, Karachi.
After 9/11 the West and a handful of Muslim countries were in the grips of terrorists. People in the name of Islam were committing atrocities that would pale into insignificance with the massacres of Genghis Khan. Scholars and politicians were afraid of speaking out against them.

But Mufti Muneeb published a Fatwa condemning the terrorist attacks and went a step further to unite the scholars of different schools of thought from Salafis to Shias and from Deobandi to Ahl la Hadith to endorse his Fatwa. Fifty nine Dar-al Iftas heeded his call. In doing so he not only united many religious factions but made it easy for the Pakistani Authorities to speak out against the terrorists and take a firm stand against them.

Mufti Muneeb-ur-Rehman champions working within the framework of authority. He respects authority and promotes working within the bounds of the law. He writes a lot; with a hawk's eye he scours the liberal writers who ignorantly write about or against Islamic values and challenges them. So, his writing is about correcting the mistakes and the views of misinformed social commentators.

Several national papers publish his columns regularly and they are very popular. He writes like a reformer with a sense of responsibility of getting things right, challenging falsehood and evil. He freely shares his wisdom and wit with politicians, journalists, diplomats and the ordinary citizens. He has established himself as a fearless and formidable scholar who is willing to take serious risks and stand up for truth and justice.

He explains in a column on "The cry of Ramadan" that since the beginning of independent TV channels no one has evaluated their benefit or harm to our society. One clear benefit of independent TV channels has been to tackle corruption, consequently the politicians are fearful of it. However, he laments the excessive sensationalism for the sake of viewer ratings. But he reserves his core criticism "the violation of the sanctity of the holy month of Ramadan." He points out how the spiritual month which should be a devotional time of moral flourishing has been commoditised for advertising revenues.

He expertly explains the jurisprudence and the legal system of Islam with exceptional rigour and clarity. This is reflected in the collection of his Fatwas in Urdu; religious edicts that he has been issuing since 1985, the Tafheem al Masail. Currently it has 13 volumes spread over thousands of pages. In these pages he tackles diverse subjects from Wudu to witchcraft and interest to insurance.

His style is rigorous delving deep into the minutia of the classical grammarians to the complex principles of the Usulees, the experts of Jurisprudence.

He has an extensive network of former students. Hundreds of young men who studied in his seminary, Jamia Naeemia in Karachi. These students are now senior Imams in major masjids, others are professors in colleges and universities. Some are founders and leaders of Islamic organisations, from Kashmir to Durban in South Africa, New York to Walthamstow, London and every major city. This gives Mufti Muneeb-ur-Rehman amazing influence over millions of Muslims globally.

Mufti Muneeb lives with simplicity, preferring the Prophetic way. For sixty years he has been the Imam of the Masjid al-Aqsa in Karachi. This shows the man's stability and loyalty. He is firmly grounded. When his son died of cancer at the young age of 36, he was naturally distraught but remained patient in the time-honoured way, fasabrun jameelun, no complaints, only submission. There was a crowd of sixty thousand at the funeral, everyone mourning. Mufti Sahib asked them all, in a dignified way, "for decades I have prayed for you, today I ask you to pray for my beloved son." In countless small acts of generosity Mufti Sahib has forged human links with ordinary students to powerful rulers.
 He is an agent of renewal, for him the sense of Islamic history is palpable and real. The life and the message of the benefactor of humanity, the beloved Messenger ﷺ is a transcendental experience for him. He believes in the message that humanity is truly Khlifat-ullah, the caretakers of the world.

Mufti Muneeb-ur-Rehman has written a book that is about delicate and serious subjects, the corruption of religious practices and playing with theology. He has fused scholarly observations with wrenching criticisms of the innovators. He challenged those who have spiced spiritual poetry recital with drums and tambourines; he scorned the charlatans who claim to be spiritual guides but flout the Shariah; he has attacked the liberal secular journalist who mocked the Islamic symbols; he has warned the masses to be careful of the fake scholars. He is a serious scholar who writes without fear or favour, a writer who dissolves the delusions of religious fanatics and the misinformation of the secular liberals with a unique style. It is a book that is painful and intellectually challenging to read.

Painful to read because who could believe that sacred practices would be tampered with? who could desecrate holy activities? Sometimes his writing sounds hostile, but for the Mufti it is a religious duty. He believes that from within and without there are serious challenges and troublesome developments that must be reformed. So, he takes his pen and paper and scrolls a rebuttal, it seems hostile, but this is an act of benevolence because he is reforming and correcting those who are mistaken, with a pen not a gun or a bomb. He uses reason and sound judgement backed by Divine writ. That is why no one can accuse him of being unreasonable. His is a civilised way of arguing. *"Invite to your Lord's way wisely: teaching in a pleasant manner and debating with courtesy; your Lord knows the one who strayed from his way in the one guided"* (Al-Nahl: 125).

He is a dyed-in-the-wool conservative scholar staunchly opposed to the secular liberal values. He thinks that secularism poses a threat to the Islamic religious culture of Pakistan, but he regards the real threat comes from within. Due to the excesses of the charlatans, poorly educated preachers and uncanny innovators. There is growing cynicism in the masses. He thinks that we need to take a harder look at our priorities to recover our credibility of being the reasonable, moderate and caring Pakistanis. He says there is a crisis of trust, people are walking away from the masjid and the mimber, the pulpit. There is a growing generation who is cynical about the way Muslims are behaving and believe that Islam is now another means to some other end. We must rescue Islam from these people.

These scholars are an asset of the Ahl As-Sunnah Wal-Jamaah. We are grateful to them for their cooperation and pray for them. We request them to consider this reformation and guide us with their expertise. They are our partners in this wonderful mission and thereby earn Divine reward. We request wealthy people to help us to distribute this book widely. Muslim organisations and charities should consider running courses for their staff on this brief book of 11 chapters.

We have inherited this passion for Islam and our school of thought from Ala-hazrat Maulana Ahmed Raza Khan Qadri (Ala-hazrat). We pray to Allah to raise his station in Paradise.

In the past few decades some members of the Ahl As-Sunnah wal-Jamaah have adopted sluggishness and indifference with respect to some practices. They have abandoned religious obligations and in the name of 'love of the Messenger' started peculiar practices. This is unacceptable as it undermines the integrity of Ahl As-Sunnah Wal-Jamaah and will lead to its downfall. A Persian couplet expresses the enraged feelings:

> 'Ahl As-Sunnah Wal-Jamaah's wretched state has angered me
> were I to say those things my tongue would go up in flames;
> Were I to keep them secret in my bosom, I fear my bone marrow
> would become like boiling water'

It's time to stop compromising, it's time to provide clear proofs so that people can be safe from innovations and succeed in their religious duties. We are doing this because we are accountable to Allah. We humbly request the readers to pray for us to be audacious and sincere.

Chapter 1:
The first responsibility of the scholars is to reform beliefs and practices

The beliefs and practices established by the texts (Quran and the Sunnah) cannot be replaced by weaker texts. So, the consensus or the majority's judgements cannot be overturned by rare and weak judgements. The scholars consider this innovation (Bidah). This misleads people and creates conflict. The Quran states, *"He is the one who revealed the book to you: some of its verses are precise in meaning, they are the foundation stone of the book whilst others are ambiguous. The people whose minds are sick chase after what is ambiguous, they want to stir up disagreement and to concoct their own interpretations; yet only Allah knows their exact meaning, and those firmly grounded in knowledge say "we believe in it, since all of it is from our Lord," only those with understanding pay heed"* (Ale Imran: 7).

Badawi said, "Allah says that these people chase the meanings of ambiguous verses and take their literal meanings or interpret them wrongly to sow doubts in people's minds, to confuse them with vague meanings. They want to prove that ambiguous verses contradict the decisive verses and thereby interpret the ambiguous verses as they like." This view of the ambiguous verses of the Quran is the view held by the classical commentators of the Quran including, Baghawi, Ibn Kathir and Suyuti. For example, Ibn Kathir wrote, "in the ambiguous verses they find an opportunity to misinterpret them. They use them as evidence to prove their fake arguments because they see a slight probability in them for their ulterior purpose (Ibn Kathir: Vol. 1 Pg 478). Elsewhere he said, "It is such places where these misguided people have slipped" (Al-Bidaya wal-Nihaya: Vol. 5 Pg 248).

The difference between decisive meaning and misguided interpretation

The decisive or definitive verses of the Quran are those whose meanings are clear and fixed so that they do not require interpretation. The Laws of Shariah, the do's and don'ts; the fundamental beliefs are established from these verses. Decisive laws are also based on the Sunnah, the consensus and the majority's judgement. In contrast, relying on judgements that are anomalous, weak, rejected and unacceptable will lead to conflict. It sows doubts in people's minds about the truth. Ala-Hazrat wrote "there are only a few judgements against which you cannot find an anomalous statement. Most sound and acceptable judgements which we take for granted as truth if you search hard-enough you can find weak, rejected and deviant proof against them. Books are full of rejected, right and wrong kind of evidence. But those people who are intelligent and possess Allah's guidance will be able to separate the right from the wrong and good from the bad. They can sort out wheat from the chaff! Otherwise, people will remain confused. If I wasn't afraid of the devious and misguided lot, I would have presented examples to prove my point. What can we do? Some people revel in searching for the false and are busy in unnecessary debates, "the people whose minds are sick chase after what is ambiguous, they want to stir up disagreement and to concoct their own interpretations".[1]

Once this principle is understood you will see why some rhetoric published by the secular-liberal lobbies is based on these confused and weak discourses. Seyeda Aisha the mother of the believers said, "the Messenger ﷺ read this verse of Ale Imran and remarked "Aisha! When you meet such people, who are chasing the interpretation of such verses then know these are the same people who Allah is talking about in this verse".[2]

In the name of Sufism some non-religious, non-practicing charlatan Pirs[3] prevent their followers from learning religious knowledge. They argue against seeking the knowledge of Shariah, yet the evidence for the learning of Shariah is overwhelming. They want people to stay ignorant and empty of knowledge, so their trade continues. This is the enemy within who causes damage, they camouflage themselves. Previously this sect was called the Hamiyah, Shaykh Abdul Qadir Jilani wrote about them in the 13th century, "the people of Hamiyah sect oppose the seeking of sciences of Shariah and forbid its teaching. They follow the philosophers who believe that the Quran is a veil. Poetry is the

---

[1] Matla-al Qamarain: 71
[2] Bukhari: 4547
[3] Pir is a Persian title for a spiritual guide following a set spiritual order.

Quran of Hamiyah, so they encourage the learning of poetry. They even ignore the established prayer-formulas because of these beliefs, they are ruined, they call themselves Ahl As-Sunnah Wal-Jamaah but they are not, they also call themselves Qalandari and Haidari".[4]

Their claim to be the followers of Maula Ali is false, since Ali was the ocean of knowledge, the gate of the city of knowledge and the perfect manifestation of the sheer beauty and perfection of the blessed Messenger ﷺ Mustafa. The deviant people with their trickery want to keep their followers away from scholars through their net of lies like: Shariah and Tariqa are two separate entities, therefore the scholars of Shariah cannot get on with the scholars of Tariqah. They believe Shariah is for those who haven't got the Haqiqa yet. Ala-Hazrat wrote a monograph, "The sayings of the Gnostics in praise of scholars of Shariah". Here are a few quotes from this monograph:

a) The view that Shariah is the name of laws: the obligatory, the necessary, the permissible and the forbidden; the rules concerning body and the soul: heart and the mind; all the sciences of gnosis; these are parts of the Shariah. The consensus among the friends of Allah is that all the realities must be judged through the prism of Shariah. If they comply with Shariah they are acceptable and valid but if they are against the Shariah they are rejected and unacceptable in fact, they are contemptable. So Shariah is the foundation and the standard. Shariah means "the path" the path of the beloved Muhammad ﷺ. This is definitive and absolute. It is not just a set of laws about rituals. It is the path. Allah orders us to pray five times a day and in every unit of it he orders us to say "O Lord, guide us on the path of Muhammad, and keep us firmly on his Shariah".[5]

b) The view that Tariqah is 'the arrival' or 'the connection' with Allah is ignorance. In Arabic Tariq and Tariqah mean the path, not 'the arrival'

---

[4] Sirrul Asrar: 58
[5] Fatawa Rizwiyya: Volume 21:523

or 'the connection'. So, the Tariqah is also 'the path'. If it is separated from Shariah then according to the Quran such Tariqah cannot be taken, as it will not lead to Allah, instead it will lead to the Satan. It will not lead to paradise but to hell. The Quran calls all paths false, except the Shariah. Therefore, the Tariqah is Shariah i.e. it is part of this brightly lit path. The separation of the Tariqah from Shariah is impossible. Anyone who considers Tariqah as separate from Shariah is breaking it from Allah's path. Nay, the true Tariqah is not the path of Iblis the rejected, it is part of the Shariah.[6]

c) The scholars of Shariah are not barriers to Tariqah, in fact they are it's guardians and doorkeepers. Yes, they are a barrier to such Tariqah that is satanic and detached from the Shariah. Even the Almighty Lord is against them. The Almighty calls such paths "rejected, unacceptable and cursed." Every Muslim needs the guidance of the scholars of Shariah at all times, particularly those who are starting on their journey of Tariqah. The Prophet likened such ignorant people who are deprived of Shariah to a blinkered donkey circling the watering well. So, if the scholars are stopping you from being a blindfolded donkey then is that a sin?"[7]

Ala Hazrat explained in detail the 10 beliefs of Ahl as-sunnah Walja'ah. He explained the tenth belief as follows:

The Tenth belief: Shariah and the Tariqah

Shariah and Tariqah are not different nor do they oppose each other. Without following the Shariah, achieving the divine pleasure is impossible. Shariah is all the laws comprising of physical, bodily, heart, mind and the sciences of gnosis. Each one of these is Tariqah. The consensus is that all the realities of the friends of Allah must be judged according to the Shariah. If they are in accordance with it, then they are acceptable, otherwise they should be rejected and regarded as despicable and devious.

---

[7] Fatawa Rizwiyya: Volume 21:535

The Quranic verse *"It is only on this straight Path that my Lord will be found"* and the other verse *"this is my straight path so follow it, and do not follow other paths that lead away from it, the Lord orders this so that you may become pious"*.[8] The Quran clearly states that Shariah is the only path whose purpose and goal is Allah through which you achieve divine proximity. Any path that will take you away from Him will not be Shariah, no matter what it is called. Tariqah is the result of the Shariah. There are many monks, Yogis and Sannyasis who do not follow Shariah but can perform weird miracles. Does that mean they are truthful? Where do they lead to? The fire of hell.[9]

The Sufi submits his desires and ego to the Shariah. The person who follows his desires and ego and neglects the Shariah cannot be a Sufi. Shariah is the food and Tariqah the energy from it. If you do not eat the food, you will not have the energy to do the good works. Shariah is the eye and the Tariqah is the sight, the power to see. If the eye is damaged, you will not see!

If there was any possibility of abandoning the Shariah after one has attained the divine proximity, so that one no longer needs to fulfil the rules of Shariah then the beloved Messenger ﷺ and Maula Ali would-be the most deserving of this relaxation in the law, but that is not the case. In fact it is the opposite, the closer you become to Allah, the more stringent the obedience of the rules of Shariah. That is why it is said "the good deeds of the righteous are the sins of the foremost" i.e. the good deeds of the pious are wonderful but compared to the foremost people they're minor. The leader of the sinless, beloved master ﷺ spent nights in vigil, staying up in worship and standing for long periods so that his feet would swell. He did this for the sake of his followers, who are obliged to pray only five daily prayers. But, because of his glorious status the night vigil (Tahajjud) was compulsory on him. Yet the night vigil is a recommended practice for the Muslims.

Junaid al-Baghdadi was asked: some people claim that following the rules of

---

[8] Al-Anam: 153
[9] Fatawa Rizwiyya: Volume 21:523

Shariah is the means to divine proximity, once we have arrived at the destination then what is the point of following the Shariah? He replied 'they speak truth. They have reached the destination but which? Hell! Even the thieves and adulterers are better than them. If I grew old and reached the age of 1,000 years, I would never abandon the rules of Shariah. I wouldn't even neglect the recommended, the voluntary or the preferable acts. All the paths are blocked, except the path trodden by the blessed Mustafa.

"Whoever travels on a path other than that of beloved Mustafa ﷺ will never reach his destination."

Insulting the Shariah is Kufr and leads to disbelief. To insult the scholars of Shariah will result in humiliation in the hereafter. To go beyond the boundaries of the Shariah is fisq and disobedience. A true Sufi considers the scholars who have correct beliefs to be the heirs, guardians and the champions of the beloved Mustafa ﷺ. So, honouring them is honouring the beloved Messenger ﷺ. Our religion is based on this reverence of the scholars and a practising scholar will show respect for a Sufi and will display humility in his presence. Since he knows the truth, he is protected by the truth and he will regard him as superior to himself and free from worldly evils.[10]

My dear, can you see how these ignorant, lazy and corrupt Pirs present poetry as evidence in opposition to the Shariah, consensus and the majority's judgement. They have memorised some stories about the pious. Stories whose authenticity is first doubtful and even if any of them are authentic, it can be interpreted. Just as we would interpret the ambiguous verses of the Quran. They ignore the venerable scholars, who have given the following rules when reading the past scriptures: we will reject anything in those scriptures that is against the Quran and Sunnah and we remain silent about anything that is neither against nor in agreement with Quran and Sunnah.

The beloved master Mustafa ﷺ wrote letters to many rulers, made treaties with

---

[10] Fatawa Rizwiyya: Volume 29:386 to 390

them and after offering them the opportunity of accepting Islam he challenged them to Jihad. He established the truth, identified the dissenters (Khawarij); the Rafadites (Shian-e-Ali): and the Fatalists (Qadriya) in order to warn us of their corrupt ways. Therefore, no scholar should compromise when tackling any of these deviant sects. Discussions must be scholarly, dignified and executed wisely to expose their deviance so that people can be protected from their misguidance. Ala-Hazrat said "countering the people of innovation is duty at the time of need." Khateeb al-Baghdadi and other experts of Hadith quote the Messenger ﷺ who said "when conflicts and innovations appear, and people insult my disciples then the scholars must defend them with their knowledge and wisdom. If anyone fails to do so, Allah, the Angels and the people will curse them; nor will their prayers be accepted".[11] The Hadith explains the responsibilities of scholars, "the best people of the future generations will take the responsibility for this knowledge. They will refute the extremists' interpolations and exaggerations, the falsehood of the fake, and the confusion of the ignorant".[12] In another Hadith the phrase "the best people of future generation will take responsibility" is replaced with "this knowledge will be inherited by". This means that the contemporary reviver of religion must conform to the teachings of the previous reviver and follow him. This implies we must avoid being negative about religious personalities, but ready to identify the innovators who spread false beliefs and practices. That is the responsibility of the reviver and the scholars of truth.

---

[11] Fatawa Rizwiyya: Volume 27:11
[12] Mishkat: 248, Sharh Mishkat al-Asar

Chapter 2:
The reformation of Takfir and issuing Fatwa of Kufr

The excommunication of a Muslim by issuing a fatwa

la-Hazrat wrote "there are four definitively established levels of the Shariah:

1) The necessities of religion: these are established by the Quran, the mass reported Ahadith and consensus. These are established by definitive texts and there is no doubt and any other interpretation will be deemed false and denial is Kufr.

2) The necessities of the school of Ahl As-Sunnah Wal-Jamaah: here, the evidence comes from the definitive texts but there is slight doubt in their certainty being absolute. Therefore, their denial is not Kufr but considered misguidance.

3) Thabitat-e-Muhkamat: the evidence is presumptive (Zanni) or weak and it is based on Ahadith reported by a single narrator where the hadith is either Sahih (sound) or Hassan (acceptable). Similarly, the statements of the majority of scholars can be evidence for Thabitat-e-Muhkamat, because "the hand of Allah is over the community." So, their denial is considered sinful and mistaken but is not declared misguided or Kafir.

4) Zanniyat-e-Muhtamalah, the mere assumptions: to prove a concept one requires strong proofs and of course opposite views exist. Their denier is considered mistaken but not as a Kafir or a sinner."

To challenge and dispute any of these four levels of Shariah, the evidence must be of the same level. Only an ignorant person will demand an evidence of a higher level. There is a time for everything, every point has a specific place. A proof for a claim ought to be at the same level and should match it. The person who denies this principle is called "Zindeeq", liberal, freethinker.[13]

---

[13] Fatawa Rizwiyya: Volume 29:385

The difference between Kufr Luzoomi and Iltizami; the two types of Disbelief

1) The disbelief of the Jews, Christians, Hindus, Sabiens, Zoroastrians and the idolaters is proven from the Quran and the disbelief of the Buddhists, Jains and atheists et cetera. from deductive proofs of the text.

2) A person who claims to be a Muslim but denies or mocks any of the definitively established beliefs - that form the necessity of religion - will become Kafir. This is Kufr Iltizami. For example, denying the finality of the prophet, the hereafter, the punishment of the hereafter, the gatherings of the day of judgement, insulting any of the prophet or slandering Seyeda Aisha the mother of believers, or regarding the Quran as a changed manuscript of Usman, to regard a non-prophet as superior to a Prophet, or regard the killing of a Muslim permissible, to mock Islamic worship like prayer, fasting and pilgrimage. Or indeed to hold any belief that opposes the Islamic beliefs contained in the authentic books of Doctrine and Fiqh.

3) Luzoom-e-Kufr: This is indirect denial of any necessities of religion. When the evidence is put together and sequenced against such a person it would ultimately lead to the denial of a necessity of religion. Some jurists in this case will pronounce the Kufr. However, the cautionary position is to make him repent and to refresh the faith. But he cannot be called Kafir. If there is the slightest room for an alternative interpretation, then pronouncing Kufr should be avoided, so he isn't excommunicated. It is wrong to condemn someone without giving him the benefit of the doubt, particularly if this is done to incite people against him or to please the public opinion. The position of Ahl As-Sunnah Wal-Jamaah is to be extremely careful about excommunicating anyone until their Kufr is clearly established. The adversaries of Ahl As-Sunnah Wal-Jamaah are the ones who do such things. We should follow our venerable fathers and be careful about pronouncing someone's Kufr.

Ala-Hazrat wrote a book to rebut 'Taqwiyaut-ul Iman' by Ismail Dehlavi. He enumerated 70 points of Kufr, but when he heard that Ismail Dehlavi had repented, he declined to excommunicate him. He wrote "this judgement was about foolish utterances, may Allah bless the scholars who looked at everything. Despite being persecuted, scoffed and called Kafir by the misguided group."

4) Calling a Muslim 'Kafir' is a major sin according to the Hadith, its burden of Kufr will fall on him. When the Muftis judge a statement about Kufr they often mean Luzoom-e-Kufr. Until the offender is summoned and interrogated, he cannot be excommunicated. We advise that other Muftis should be consulted. Preachers who are not qualified Muftis should not give fatwa, certainly not on Kufr, even if it is only verbal. If they do not stop this, they will be in breach of the Hadith "anyone who wrongly targets someone with Kufr, will have to bear its consequences."[14] Some people want to condemn and catch out well-established personalities. Firstly, they do not fully grasp the text since they are interested in finding mistakes, yet they should be giving him the benefit of the doubt and find an alternative interpretation. We must have a good opinion of our Muslim brothers and it is imperative that we interpret the rulings correctly. The slandering of established personalities is wrong. It is not allowed. One way to give the benefit of the doubt is to interpret this as a possible addition by others, or it was appendixed by someone else later.

5) Western powers in the recent past have tried to prevent the scholars from endorsing the truth and falsifying the falsehood. They do this by supporting Muslim groups who follow the policy "we agree with all". Since the last two decades, after 9/11 they have used the veil of terrorism to force Muslims to abandon Jihad. We can not be the supporters of such groups, because Jihad is part of the Shariah. It's conditions are explained in the books of Fiqh.

---

[14] Abu Dawud: 3657

Similarly, it is unacceptable to believe that the Jews and the Christians of the Prophet's time were Kafir but today they are not. This is pointless confusion. The notion that the disbelievers and the idolaters are one group, whilst the Jews and the Christians are another group included among the believers is mistaken. This kind of interpretation is against the Quran and the Sunnah. It is unacceptable. In Surat Al-Bayyinah the people of the book are included among the disbelievers. This is the unanimous belief of the Ummah. Ibn Hajjar Al Makki wrote "anyone who doesn't regard the disbelievers and the followers of other religions like the Christians and the Jews Kafir or regards their religion to be truth is a Kafir".[15]

Guidelines for expelling someone from Ahl As-Sunnah Wal-Jamaah

1) Consensus is the unanimous agreement of the scholars therefore it forms proof and judgement and its denial is disbelief, Kufr. The Hadith, "whoever dissented has fallen into the hell".[16] The advocates of liberalism begin their attack on Islam by denying consensus. Anyone who denies consensus and thinks himself better than those illustrious sages of Islam is denying Islamic proofs. He creates conflict in the community. The self-proclaimed prophet of Qadiyan (the founder of the Ahmadiyya) used this deceitful method. To quote Ibn Hisham and Ibn Asakir in opposition to the Quran, Sunnah and the consensus is forbidden. To cite weak arguments and one's own concept of love instead of the well-established principles of Shariah is wrong. This is like pulling down the building of religion, it weakens people's trust of the Shariah and the established practices.

2) The Ahl As-Sunnah Wal-Jamaah have distinguished themselves from the Rafidite Shias in the following manner: "they regard Abu Bakr and Umar superior over all the disciples, they love Usman and Ali and wipe the moccasins".[17] To think of another model of the disciples' superiority

[15] Al-Ilam Biqawat al-Islam: 164
[16] Al-Mustadrik: 390
[17] Sharh-e-Aqaid Al-Nasafi: 150

is against the beliefs of Ahl As-Sunnah Wal-Jamaah imam Al-Azam wrote "the best human being after the beloved Messenger ﷺ is Abu Bakr".[18]

Tafdeelis are excluded from the Ahl As-Sunnah Wal-Jamaah

It is a consensual belief of the Ahl As-Sunnah Wal-Jamaah that Abu Bakr is the best human being after the Prophet. To regard another disciple, even if that is Umar, Usman or Ali, is to walk into the valley of Rafidites[19] (an extremist sect of the Shias). Ala-Hazrat was asked "Zaid's mother believes there is no disciple who is equal to the rank of Ali," he replied "Zaid's mother is outside the pale of Ahl As-Sunnah Wal-Jamaah and is a member of the misguided sect of the Tafdeelis. The Imams consider them as smaller brothers of Rafidites. Similarly, the statement that "Abu Bakr was the Messenger's political heir and Ali was his spiritual heir", is against the views of the majority of Ahl As-Sunnah Wal-Jamaah. Such a statement must be rejected as it supports the Tafdeeli view.

Ala-Hazrat wrote a monograph to prove 'the superiority of Abu Bakr and Umar.' He said "Sunniyat is the name of the straight path that remains pure from the extremes of high and low. Allah Almighty said, *"he did not make it crooked"*.[20] Since we have condemned the Tafdeelis, it is fair to challenge the latter-day Indian writers from the other extreme as they believe that Abu Bakr and Umar are superior in all aspects. This is an erroneous view. Once the suspicions of both sides are cleared, we will better understand the meaning of Tafdeeli. We have established above that because of a single superior character trait one doesn't become 'superior', this will contradict the fact that each disciple had some special trait that others lacked. Some disciples had traits that even the four Caliphs didn't have. This doesn't make the individual better than them. This is against the consensus. Let us investigate the books of Hadith, it is clear that the Almighty Lord blessed Maula Ali with amazing blessings which others did not receive. Who can deny the shining sun? Our beloved master ﷺ is honoured with "we raised your honour". It is impossible for us to enumerate all his

---

[18] Sharh Mullah Ali Qari: 61
[19] Fatawa Rizwiyya: Volume 21: 152
[20] Al-Kahf: 4

greatness, the splendidness and uniqueness because they are so numerous. We do not have the capability to comprehend them. Those who believe in the superiority of Abu Bakr and Umar in all aspects should know that the Prophet ﷺ spoke highly of Ali.

> 1) Jabir ibn Abdullah narrated I heard the Messenger ﷺ say, "People come from different branches of their lineage, but Ali and I are from the same branch." (Tabarani Ausat: 4150)
> 2) Umar reported I heard the Messenger ﷺ say, "every child's lineage comes from the father except for the children of Fatima, my daughter, I will be their father".[21]

Ala Hazrat paid tribute to Maula Ali in Matal al-Qamarian, page 68. I will paraphrase it here. 'Absolute superiority' is attributed to Abu Bakr and Umar. However, some disciples were blessed with unique qualities and Maula Ali is the most distinguished amongst them. No fair-minded person can deny it. What is meant by 'absolute superiority'? When someone asks, 'who is the superior disciple?' The answer will be "Abu Bakr", this should be understood in the positive sense not negative. So 'absolute superiority' and 'superiority in some respects' are not the same things. He said "most spiritual orders trace their origin to the blessed Messenger ﷺ through Maula Ali. Everyone agrees about this. However, Ala-Hazrat doesn't agree with this point of view, since this necessitates the division of Khilafa into two parts: the temporal rulership and spiritual mastery. He regards this against the beliefs of Ahl As-Sunnah Wal-Jamaah and rejects it with strong arguments. The people who hold this binary division of the Khilafa are called Sanafadiyah. They deceptively turned a clear belief of the Ahl As-Sunnah Wal-Jamaah into a confused viewpoint. Similarly, it is not inconsistent to love the inferior, he can be loved as much as the superior. When Maula Ali asked the Messenger ﷺ about Fatima "is she dearer to you than me" he replied, "she's dearer than you but you are dearer than her".[22]

---

[21] Tabarani Al- Kabir: 2631
[22] Musnad Humaidi: 38

The city of Makkah is superior in terms of the reward for worship in Masjid al-Haram, but the city of Madinah is dearer. He prayed for it to become the dearest. No one can doubt that his prayer has been accepted.

The signs of hypocrisy

The practice of Ahl As-Sunnah Wal-Jamaah is to make judgement after gathering all the evidence and avoiding extremes of lows and highs. The four signs of hypocrisy are:

The first sign of hypocrisy
The hatred of the Messenger ﷺ of Allah, Surat al-Munafiqun was revealed about the hypocrites, they were worse than the disbelievers.

The second sign of hypocrisy
The hatred of the rightly guided Caliphs. The Messenger ﷺ said, "love of Abu Bakr and Umar is sign of faith and their hatred is sign of hypocrisy".[23] The Messenger ﷺ once refused to lead the funeral prayer of a man who was unfriendly to Usman.[24]

"The love of the Ansar (disciples who were resident of Madinah) is a sign of faith and their hatred is a sign of hypocrisy".[25]

The Messenger ﷺ said, "Be careful about my disciples, do not make them targets of criticism after me; anyone who loves them, loves them because of me; anyone who hates them, hates them because of me; anyone who insults them insults me; anyone who insulted me has angered Allah and anyone who angered Allah will be punished".[26]

---

[23] Fazal-e-Sahaba; Ahmed ibn Hanbal: 487
[24] Tirmadhi: 3709
[25] Bukhari: 17; Muslim: 235
[26] Tirmadhi: 3862

Third sign of hypocrisy
The hatred of Maula Ali and the Prophet's family. The Messenger ﷺ said, "only a believer will love Ali and only a hypocrite will hate Ali".[27]
"Love for me demands the love of my family".[28]
"It is obligatory to love Abu Bakr, Umar, Usman and Ali".[29]

The fourth sign of hypocrisy
"He is not trustworthy, he lies, breaks promises and curses when arguing".[30]
The Messenger ﷺ said, "when you have the four qualities of honesty, strong character, truthfulness and a lawful livelihood you do not need to worry about losing material goods".[31]

The respect of the Prophets family and the disciples is compulsory

The tradition of Ahl As-Sunnah Wal-Jamaah is to love the rightly guided Caliphs; the ten disciples given good news of paradise; all members of the Prophets family; the mothers of the believers; all the disciples. We praise them and love them. The praise of one is not an affront to the other, but when praising one disciple it's better that others are mentioned with courtesy. This couplet sums it up:

"The Ahl As-Sunnah reached the shores, the disciples are
their stars and the Prophet's family their ship"

The respect of elders is a cherished tradition of the Ahl As-Sunnah Wal-Jamaah. Some people attach themselves to one and mislead simple minded folks with poems and odes. According to the Quran the respect of all the Prophets is compulsory, yet they have different ranks, some higher than others. Despite that none can be ignored. Similar variation is found in the disciples ranks, none can be shunned.

---

[27] Muslim: 240
[28] Tirmadhi: 3789
[29] Tabaqat Hanabila: 1:82
[30] Bukhari: 34; Muslim: 210
[31] Ahmed: 1770

The preachers of Ahl As-Sunnah Wal-Jamaah must teach the agreed-upon beliefs and established truths. The superiority of one personality should not be exaggerated such that it lowers others, whether metaphorically, metonymically or figuratively. This would lead to the fracturing of the community and trigger conflict, so it must be avoided. However, if someone has an inclination, a special attachment with a personality it should be kept private. In public one must follow the traditions of the Ahl As-Sunnah Wal-Jamaah. Therefore, respect the venerable scholars of the past and avoid sowing seeds of conflict. We know some scholars hold unique views of some personalities and that shouldn't be discussed publicly in a negative way.

Chapter 3:
The reformation of Milad gatherings and processions

The beloved Messenger's ﷺ birth and prophetic mission are the greatest gifts from the Almighty Lord. The Quran presents him:

- *As the greatest gift and favour of the Lord for humanity and the believers.*[32]
- *Commands to rejoice when receiving God's grace and kindness.*[33]
- *Commands to constantly mention the gifts we receive, "if you have got it, flaunt it".*[34]

These verses point to the amazing standing of the beloved Messenger ﷺ who the Quran declares as a special gift of Allah. It pays special homage to him. He was also grateful to Allah for the favours and honours bestowed on him and he humbly expressed those Divine favours frequently.

Faith demands we rejoice and celebrate the birth and the coming of our Master. It is a way of displaying our love for him. Historically, Milad has been part of the religious milieu of Ahl As-Sunnah Wal-Jamaah and by the grace of Allah continues today and will remain so until the final day. Last year I published a fatwa in the national newspapers "innovations and bad practices in the gatherings of Milad". It received a lot of coverage on social media too. I discussed the permissibility of Milad gatherings and processions and I clarified two important features of the Milad: Firstly, Milad is neither included in the necessities of religion nor in the necessities of the school of thought of Ahl As-Sunnah Wal-Jamaah. However, in Pakistan and other Muslim countries it is celebrated as a national festival and a holiday in the Islamic calendar. We believe Milad is good and permissible if it remains free of unlawful innovations and bad practices.

Secondly, I discussed its purpose, which is the expression of love and reverence for our master Muhammad ﷺ therefore it is naturally a part of our faith. Allah Almighty said *"So, people! believe in Allah and his Messenger, support him and*

---

[32] Ale-Imran: 164
[33] Yunus: 58
[34] Al-Duha:10

honour him. And glorify Allah morning and evening".[35] Therefore, banning Milad is tantamount to stopping people from supporting and honouring the Messenger. The permissibility of Milad has been presented by some major figures of the Deoband School. Unfortunately, nowadays they no longer support it and in fact some criticise it, calling it idolatry and innovation. Perhaps this is due to the influence of the Salafi-Wahabi movement on the school of Deoband. It does make you wonder why this change?

The Beloved Messenger ﷺ fasted on Monday and when asked about this, he replied "I was born on this day, I announced my Prophethood on this day and the first revelation of the Quran came down on this day".[36]

Maulana Waheed-uzaman Kanpuri a scholar of the Ahl al-Hadith wrote: "from this Hadith a group of scholars conclude that to celebrate the birth of the Prophet by holding gatherings of Milad is permissible as long as the purpose is to inspire people to learn about his character and mission. These gatherings must remain free of innovation and bad practices. They are blessed, if they are seeking the truth. However, these gatherings did not take place in the time of the Messenger ﷺ or the disciples".[37]

How best to express love for the Prophet ﷺ ?

The expression of love for the Prophet must follow the teachings of Islam. The innovations will ruin this wonderful spiritual ritual and bad practice like presenting fabricated stories, hanging up unacceptable pictures in the mosques, mixed gatherings of men and women or dancing and clapping will invalidate its blessings. In some places Milad has become a commercial event; the Na'at reciters are booked through agents who take commissions. Some Na'at reciters sing like pop singers often using tambourines and drums. Wealthy people distribute heaps of sweets and cakes for personal popularity. This makes a mockery of such a spiritual gathering. These practices must be stopped, I have

[35] Al-Fath:10
[36] Muslim: 2739
[37] Lughat ul-Hadith: vol 2:119

asked my fellow Muftis to counter these bad practices and speak out against them. (Below, we will talk more about receiving remuneration for preaching)

We understand how important it is to reform beliefs if they deviate from the mainstream. But by putting emphasis on this, the aim is not to minimise the importance of such events. These celebrations have been part of our religious milieu for a millennium. The public must know that a strong belief by itself will not get you into Paradise, you will still need good deeds. The Quran often speaks about faith and good deeds together. Of course, faith is the condition for the acceptance of deeds and for the protection from hell. For faith and piety to exist, God consciousness is necessary and the two make us trust God's kindness. This will take us to Paradise without suffering the punishment of hell. Yes, some sinful Muslims will go to hell before they enter Paradise. The punishment of Hell should not be taken lightly, the Prophet 🕌 said, "the minimum punishment of hell will be this, a person will wear heated sandals, that will make the brain boil." May Allah protect all from this punishment and grant us the intercession of our beloved Messenger 🕌 so that we may enter Paradise without giving account.

Slogans and mottos are part of our culture, but the life of the Messenger 🕌 and his disciples was more than that. It was faith with actions and sacrifices. Unfortunately, some people pay scant attention to that. The Prophet's life in Makkah was focused on teaching and preaching but he also suffered at the hands of his opponents who mocked and scoffed him. In the small town of Taif, near Makkah, he was pelted with stones as he preached.

In his Madani life he was occupied in worship, preaching, teaching, high level diplomacy and the dispensing of justice. He was engaged in the military campaigns like Badr, Uhud, Ahzab, the Treaty of Hudabiya, the conquest of Makkah, Khaybar and expeditions to Tabuk and Hunain et cetera. He made more than 25 expeditions in the 10 years of Madani life.

Gatherings are an important part of the social fabric of any religious community, the Milad gatherings are a means of spiritual enlightenment and moral inspiration. Certain people have influenced them to such an extent that now the Milad gathering is a Na'at gathering. In such gatherings professional singers perform in an outlandish way, neither seeking the divine pleasure nor inspiring the public. Their aim is to make money, which is apparent from their stylish outfits and celebrity status. The manners of Milad gatherings are ignored: credible scholars are not invited to speak and if they are, they're given the minimum of time at the beginning or the end, when the majority of the audience have not yet arrived or have left. The centre stage is taken by the Na'at performers, some of whom do not have the beliefs of the Ahl As-Sunnah Wal-Jamaah, some are pro-Rafidites and some have poor character. So, Milad gatherings have turned into a glittering show, lacking faith, spirituality or the love of Allah and the Messenger ﷺ.

I also criticise them for wasting money on publicity. This money was raised to spread the love of the beloved Messenger ﷺ. We believe wasting money on this type of marketing is unacceptable, instead it should be spent on charitable causes that comply with the Messenger's ﷺ mission.

The reformation of Na'at recital

Na'at is a special genre of poetry in which the poet praises and pays homage by relating the beautiful qualities of the beloved Messenger ﷺ. The Composing and the recital of Na'at is the Sunnah of God and the Messenger ﷺ himself. Convening gatherings of Na'at has been at the heart of Muslim culture and at the heart of Ahl As-Sunnah Wal-Jamaah. It is a blessed activity and a holy gathering, disciplined by manners.

The purpose of organising Na'at gatherings is to grow the love of the beloved Messenger ﷺ, to reform oneself and to become an obedient servant of Allah and his Messenger. Therefore, in the gatherings of Milad the laws of Shariah must not be flouted. Mixed gatherings, tambourine, drum and commercial razzmatazz is forbidden. The great saint of Lahore, Syed Ali Hujwari wrote "the ignorant people have adopted the outward practice and ignored the purpose hence ruined themselves and the audience".[38]

The Recital of the Quran in which singers are imitated is disliked. The beloved Messenger ﷺ said "read the Quran with the Arab accent and pronunciation, do not read it like the Jews and the Christians read their scripture. After me there will come people who will read it with musical tones and like the mourners, their reading will remain in their throat it won't touch their hearts, they and their audience will be tried".[39]

The majority of the scholars do not allow Na'at recital with tambourine and drum. Allama Mullah Ali Qari said "it is disbelief to read the Quran with tambourine and drum. I believe that it applies to the recital of Na'at and Zikr of Allah with clapping".[40]

Performing the Zikr of Allah with Music

It is commonly seen that Na'at singers are flanked by boys on the right and the left singing the divine names. They mispronounce the Divine names and that is a sad scene that is staged in Masjids up and down the country. It is not permissible. The mispronunciation of the Divine names is forbidden. They are not glorifying Allah but rather their purpose is to create the sensation of the drumbeats. Indeed, sometimes they achieve this by turning on the echo in the sound system, which also creates drumbeats. This is not permissible.

It is forbidden to call someone a sinner in controversial matters

It is not permissible to label someone as a 'major sinner' or Fasiq in matters where the scholars' views differ. For example, the use of musical instruments in Qawwali and the devotional singing common among the Sufis of the Indian subcontinent. This has been a matter of dispute for over 900 years.

---

[38] Kashaf al-Mahjub: 452
[39] Mishkat: 2207
[40] Al-Fiqh al-Kabir:167

The scholars who quote Ahadith to support their argument take the judgement from the Ahadith as absolute, therefore they forbid the use of musical instruments. The scholars on the other side interpret these Ahadith differently: they say that Qawwali is not the same as amusement and frivolity. Their argument is that when a judgement is applied to a derivative of the word, its infinitive needs to be understood. The infinitive of amusement in Arabic is 'Malahi' (frivolous, deflects the attention). Therefore, this judgement only applies to these musical instruments when they are used for amusement and deflect attention from Allah's remembrance.

One group regards it as forbidden whilst the other as permissible. The former says, it is forbidden but refrain from calling the opponents sinners, thus showing mutual respect. An example of this is Ala-Hazrat and the spiritual guides, the Pirs of Kuchcha Sharif in India. Ala-Hazrat regards the use of musical instruments forbidden but the Pirs of Kuchcha Sharif are relaxed about them and they listen to Qawwali with musical instruments. Ala-Hazrat respected them yet when it came to sinners, he was very harsh about them.

The Pirs of the Chishti order like to listen to Qawwali if it is free from unlawful wordings and meets the conditions of religious gatherings. They do not allow the mixing of men and women nor singers who are sinners and deviant, nor do they allow the reading of poems that flout Shariah laws.

The differences of opinions among credible and influential scholars today is friendly and can be compared to the differences among the early jurists including the four Imams of the Ahl As-Sunnah Wal-Jamaah. Despite major differences they were friendly and respectful and they never insulted nor held others in contempt. We notice a similar kind of relationship among the Pirs of the different spiritual orders. Mufti Sharif Amjadi wrote "when the scholars of Ahl As-Sunnah Wal-Jamaah differ on a matter of Fiqh, it is not right to call anyone a sinner. The scholars of Kuchcha Sharif are very dear and trustworthy scholars yet they listen to Qawwali accompanied by an Oboe. Their argument is "that the use of the Oboe is forbidden for listening to frivolous songs." So, their view is that anyone who listens with the intention of amusement and frivolity is forbidden, but anyone who listens to music with the intention of gaining divine nearness then it is permissible. However, we don't agree with this viewpoint, because the Hadith strictly forbids the use of an Oboe, and it cannot be made into a specific case. Since the other side are trustworthy scholars, we cannot accuse them of being sinners. Although we will still reject their viewpoint, but we will not call them sinners.[41]

The son of Ala-Hazrat Mufti Azam Hind cancelled the judgement of Fisq against those who listen to Qawwali with music. He wrote "according to us listening to Qawwali with musical instruments is forbidden, though some scholars differ from us. We do not accept their viewpoint but will not give the Fatwa of Fisq against them. This doesn't mean we think that it is permissible to listen to Qawwali with an oboe. I believe there are two charges against them, firstly, they are doing something forbidden and secondly they regard it permissible.[42]

This is an excellent example of religious tolerance, Mufti-e-Azam did not cancel his Fatwa nor accuse the opposition of committing Fisq. This is caution, tolerance and respect for the differences of opinion.

The processions of Milad

The processions of Milad are a means of displaying 'support' and 'honouring' the beloved master ﷺ. The participants must follow the rules and manners: keeping their gaze down and engaging in the constant reading of Darud Sharif, reciting the Na'at of The Prophet and being in the state of Wudu. They should walk together with dignity in an organised way, so that onlookers admire their orderliness and good manners. Unfortunately, some processions are so badly organised they give a negative impression of Muslims and even Muslims feel ashamed.

---

[41] Fatawa Sharh Bukhari
[42] Fatawa Mustafiya: 456

Some people install models of the mosque of The Prophet and of the Ka'aba Sharif in marketplaces and they encourage people to circle them. This is not permissible. These processions are for displaying the pure feelings of love, devotion and honouring the best of Humanity ﷺ. They are a means of spreading the beautiful teachings and bringing people towards Islam. We must be creative and imaginative enough to plan strategies to inspire people but we must preserve these rituals from innovations and bad practices so that the opponents of Ahl As-Sunnah Wal-Jamaah cannot use them to criticise us.

Chapter 4:
How to safeguard the status of the beloved Messenger ﷺ ?

The Quraish of Makkah were often rude and heartless towards the Messenger ﷺ. They enjoyed spreading false propaganda against him. They mocked, scoffed and made fun of him, his religion and his followers. To counter their false propaganda the Messenger ﷺ told the disciples to start a counter campaign. He recommended they ridicule the Quraish through satire. Aisha the mother of believers said the Messenger ﷺ told us "ridicule and satirise the Quraish because that will upset them." He then summoned Ibn Rawaha and told him to ridicule them. So, he did, however the Messenger ﷺ was not satisfied with his wordings. Then he summoned Ka'ab ibn Malik and Hassan ibn Thabit. Hassan came to the Messenger ﷺ and boldly said "the time has come you have summoned the lion who will beat the enemy with his tail" and held out his tongue, "I swear by Him who sent you with the truth I will tear them to pieces with this tongue like tearing leather". On hearing this the Messenger ﷺ said "Hassan don't be too quick, remember that I am related to them – and share their lineage so before you say anything consult Abu Bakr who is the expert in their lineage." Hassan consulted Abu Bakr and came back "O Messenger ﷺ of God he has separated your lineage from them, and I swear by him who sent you with the truth I will preserve your lineage from theirs and take it out like pulling a hair from cream." Aisha said I heard the Messenger ﷺ telling Hassan "Hassan, when you were defending the status of the Messenger, Jibril stood shoulder to shoulder with you" He said, "Hassan by lampooning them you have delighted the believers and upset the disbelievers." Here is Hassan's couplet:

"O enemy of the Messenger, you criticised the status of beloved Muhammad and I have answered you and Allah will reward me". [43]

When Hassan satirised the Quraish he was safeguarding the status of the Messenger. But notice how the Messenger ﷺ told him to be careful when satirising them, effectively telling him not to be rude or offensive. There is an organised global movement against 'the safeguarding of the status of the Messenger'. Perhaps the bloggers represent the movement? Anyone who

---

[43] Muslim: 6273

stands up for the status of the blessed Messenger ﷺ through whatever means, prose or poems is doing a wonderful job. This is a true believer's sense of distinctiveness for which he is prepared to sacrifice.

The safeguarding of the status of the Messenger ﷺ is guaranteed by Clause 295 of the Pakistani Constitution. This must not be amended and any attempt to make it less effective must be resisted. For example, the stipulation that if the police officer submitting 295-C FR application must be of SSP rank or above otherwise the judge will reject it.

The bloggers

I published an article about the bloggers in a newspaper column, here is an excerpt from it:

"Blog is a website created by an individual or a group that is written in an informal or conversational style to express opinions and views." The writer of a blog is called the blogger. Over the years I have noted, with dismay, that the bloggers use harsh language and express extreme views about 'the status of the Messenger' and Islamic symbols. I find the reading of such blogs repugnant and heart-breaking. Pakistan's Ministry of Information Technology have to identify and punish them, otherwise they are complicit in the crime. Such silence is criminal."

A new law on cybercrime has been passed. As is the convention in Pakistan, laws are made to show the public that the government is doing something but they are seldom implemented nor is there an appetite to enforce them. They are bidding for time to keep the public feelings at bay. Furthermore, our politicians are obsessed with gaining the title of 'moderate' or 'liberal' in order to be accepted in Western circles. By liberal I mean people who regard themselves to be free of Islamic values, the love of the Messenger, the sanctity of the symbols of Islam and loyalty to religion and country. They criticise these values and are prepared to abandon them. Even though these are the core values of Islam. This is a very sensitive issue that must not be ignored.

The bloggers' strategy seems to be, first criticise an Islamic symbol then, ferment tension to create a tense atmosphere which incites conscientious Muslims so they react. Now label them extremists and fanatics. This will go on for days, inciting and offending them. Nothing is done to the blogger by the Pakistani authorities. If this was against the intelligence service or any other sensitive department of the government then the culprit would have gone missing or dealt with, which cannot be condoned but alas, the safeguarding of the status of the Messenger ﷺ is not important in their view, so no action is taken. There is a lot of backlash against religious extremism and rightly so but the extremism of the liberal and the secular groups goes unpunished and unnoticed.

We request the intelligence services and related departments to take immediate steps to control such incitement of hatred against Islamic symbols. Sometimes the Supreme Court of Pakistan takes notice of sensitive issues that affect the peace and security of society but they turn a blind eye to the bloggers. Is this because respectable judges do not care about the sanctity of Islamic symbols compared to other issues? We request the Chief Justice of Pakistan to take immediate action against this dangerous movement.

Another serious issue is the intra-sectarian strife that is rampant on social media. This must be stopped. We fail to understand what drives these religious zealots. According to the science of objectives of Shariah there is a principle of Sad al Zar'a: it is a strategy to stop an evil from taking place. It prevents all the prerequisites of an evil from coming together and consequently the evil action is prevented from happening. For example, the Quran said "believers, do not insult anything they worship beside Allah, otherwise they will insult Allah out of hostility and ignorance." (Al-Anam:108) This verse teaches us that if you insult their gods they will react by insulting Allah. The Messenger ﷺ said: "A major sin is to curse one's parents". The disciples were shocked "who would curse his parents?" He answered, "when someone's parents are cursed he responds by cursing the other's parents".[44] The lesson is, we must not insult

---

[44] Bukhari: 5973

other people's beloved, whether they are parents or leaders since it is human nature to react and defend their loved ones.[45]

Recommendations for the Revival of the Ahl As-Sunnah Wal-Jamaah

I recommend that Ahl As-Sunnah Wal-Jamaah make a wide-ranging strategy to defend the status of the Messenger. To achieve this goal, we must be organised. These recommendations are based on the teachings of Ala-Hazrat. He had a visionary insight and experience. The recommendations he made nearly a hundred years ago are still applicable. These recommendations reveal his passion, enthusiasm and wisdom. My purpose in presenting them is to inspire the Sunnis, what was this manifesto?

1. Empowerment of Ahl As-Sunnah Wal-Jamaah requires
a) The unity of the scholars
b) Preparedness for trials and sacrifices
c) Mobilisation of the well-off to spend for the sake of Allah

2. The establishment of quality educational institutions
a) Sponsor capable and deserving students for higher education
b) Pay good salaries to the teachers and staff
c) Assess the students' aptitude and encourage them to specialise in their chosen field. This will ensure we produce good teachers, writers, preachers and apologetics.
d) The experts specialising in Islamic studies and Arabic should be well paid and encouraged to serve Islam to their full capacity.
e) writers must be nurtured, their books published and they should be given awards to encourage them to defend the truth

3. Setting up of a think tank:
a) It's role will be to assess the needs of Ahl As-Sunnah Wal-Jamaah and formulate policies to meet those crucial needs

---

[45] Daily world 6th March 2017

b) Identify and nurture talent then motivate them to serve the Ahl As-Sunnah Wal-Jamaah.

c) Publish magazines and newspapers

d) Muslim businessmen must establish finance houses to promote Islamic finance and counter the use of usury.

Chapter 5:
The reformation of preaching and public speeches

Ignorant preachers damage the credibility of Islam

Na'at reciters and religious speakers who are not qualified scholars are a source of embarrassment and damage the credibility of Islam. The Messenger ﷺ said, "a time will come when there will be many reciters in my community but few scholars and religious knowledge will be scarce but disagreements plenty".[46]

Maula Ali asked a public speaker, "do you know the abrogating and the abrogated verses of the Quran" he replied "no", Ali said "leave the masjid and don't give a speech here again".[47]

Ala Hazrat was asked "If a person has the knowledge of Shariah, Fiqh and Islam, can he give a talk according to the verse "remind, since it benefits the believers"? He replied, "only if he is a qualified scholar, an unqualified person is not allowed to preach in public since he will cause more harm than good".[48] A lay person can read from a book written by a Sunni scholar without giving a commentary on it. In this case this would be the preaching of the author and not of the reader.

Imam Ghazali (d.1105) complained about the ignorant preachers of his time when he wrote "there is a group of preachers who have turned away from our method, only a few are saved by the divine grace from the evil of their egos, only a hand full of holy souls remain, who I know.[49]

Imagine if this was the case in the 11th century then what about the 21st century? Imam Ghazali wrote "there are public speakers who like to pick out quirky points, rhyming words and phrases, all their effort is used up on the rhyming of words rather than their meanings. They excite the public and they sing poetry about romance and separation. They create an artificial atmosphere of 'Wajad' (heightened emotions). They are Satan in human clothing and they

---

[46] Tabarani Al Kabir: 304
[47] Kanz al-Ammal: 29435
[48] Fatawa Rizwiyya: Volume 23:717
[49] Ihya Uloom Udeen 3:486

mislead people. In the past if the speaker had any shortcomings, he would still enjoin good and forbid evil, but today they set a poor example. They are deceivers since they give false hopes to their audience, their listeners are emboldened to do evil and become worldly. These public speakers dress extravagantly, ride on the well-bred horses, they are groomed from head to toe like a bride and display worldly love. They reform less but mislead the public more".[50]

On the miraculous night of the Ascension the Messenger ﷺ saw some people whose tongues were being cut with flames of fire. He was told, "these are the public speakers who created mischief among your community." Anas ibn Malik narrated "the Messenger ﷺ said, "on the night of Ascension I saw some people whose tongues were cut with scissors of fire, so I asked Jibril "who are these?" He replied, "the public speakers of your community, who enjoined good and forbid evil but didn't practise it, they read the book without understanding it".[51]

The payment for recital of Na'at

There is a growing trend to make a career out of recital of Na'at. Divine praise and Na'at of the Messenger ﷺ are for achieving divine closeness and to express one's loyalty and love. Remuneration is not allowed for carrying out the duties of Shariah except duties that require personnel like the Imam for the five daily prayers, the caller of the Azan, the teachers of the Quran, Sunnah and jurisprudence et cetera. To charge fees for the recital of Na'at is forbidden, the reciter and the organiser are sinful. Ala Hazrat said, "the fees Mr Zaid charged for Na'at performance is forbidden, it's giving and taking are both forbidden. He should promptly return it to the people from whom he took the fees. If they have died then, give it to their heirs, otherwise distribute it amongst the needy people. He must repent.[52]

---

[50] Ihya Uloom Deen 3:486
[51] Ibn Hibban 1:222
[52] Fatawa Rizwiyya: Volume 23:724

Receiving payment for public speaking

To charge fixed fees for public speaking is forbidden. Some of these preachers have a fixed rate per speech. They will not give a speech if they do not receive payment. This is a distasteful practice and it is forbidden. Ala Hazrat wrote "if the sole purpose of speaking is to get money then it is against this verse "do not sell my verses for a small price, and fear Allah."[53] This way of earning a livelihood is tainted. Particularly if they are not in need. It is like taking something forcibly from someone.[54] The second scenario is: the sole purpose of the speaker and the Na'at recital is seeking divine pleasure, but the public offer money as a gift, that is allowed. The third scenario is: the public speaker is genuinely doing it for the sake of Allah but, he is needy and would prefer to have some money. Obviously, people will pay him, although this is not as good as the second scenario it is not condemnable like the first scenario. In Durr al-Mukhtar it says, "public speakers, speaking to earn money are mistaken and represent the practice of the Jews and the Christians." This is an intermediate position between the first and the second. For example, someone goes to the pilgrimage and takes goods to sell, "there is no blame if you seek Allah's bounty." That is permissible and the jurists give the Fatwa accordingly. This is the best way to reconcile between the two scenarios.[55] The organisers of Milad gatherings must not invite Professional Na'at reciters and public speakers, instead invite those who come without the desire for money.

Avoid hiring professional master of ceremonies

The stage secretary who is sometimes called the Master of ceremonies is a new trend. It is preferable to appoint a scholar or a well-educated and well-mannered person to undertake this task. So, that he introduces the speakers. If a layman isn't allowed to give a public speech, how can he be given the authority to run an event from beginning to the end? Self-help books have been

---

[53] Al-Baqarah: 41
[54] Fatawa Alamgeeri
[55] Fatawa Rizwiyya: Volume 23:381

produced for these master of ceremonies, full of eloquent phrases and titles. The task of the master of ceremonies is simply to introduce the next speaker not to give lengthy speeches. But the professional master of ceremonies tends to take over the gathering and wastes a lot of time often reciting irrelevant poetry, fabricated stories and sometimes they even slip up and make gaffes, which then must be explained by the scholars. This undermines the authority of the Ahl As-Sunnah Wal-Jamaah. The Messenger ﷺ said, "be careful about what you attribute to me. Anyone who intentionally lied about me must reserve his place in hell and anyone who says something about the Quran from his personal opinion should do the same".[56]

Ala-Hazrat wrote "anyone who discusses Allah's being in such a manner that he commits disbelief has done something worse than adultery and theft".[57] We humbly request the Allah-fearing friends: if you are not a scholar then don't take on the role of master of ceremonies.

It is no wonder that by handing over the Milad gatherings to unqualified and careless people, the event becomes farcical and disorganised, sometimes stretching far into the night. Consequently the participants miss the morning prayer or at least fail to attend the congregation. That is clearly against the rules of Shariah. In these gatherings the Na'at reciters are seen distributing the certificates of salvation. Encouraging tardiness in religion and promoting bad deeds. Yet a true believer is always conscious of Allah and hopeful of his kindness. Allah sent his beloved Messenger ﷺ as a giver of good news and the Warner. The destination depends on the state of faith at the time of death. Ula ibn Ziyad (student of the disciple) said "you want to receive good news of paradise for your evil deeds? Yet Allah sent his Messenger ﷺ to give good news to the obedient and as a warning to the rebels".[58]

Aqaid al-Nasafi declares "to be hopeless of Allah's kindness is disbelief and to

---

[56] Tirmadhi: 2951
[57] Fatawa Rizwiyya: Volume 10:64
[58] Bukhari: 4815

feel safe from his punishment is disbelief".[59] When the sinful are not warned but given the good news of paradise then the Satan is happy as he doesn't have to do much work. Unfortunately, this kind of irresponsible talk is frequent in Na'at gatherings. I heard about a certain religious organisation that stipulated a rule for its staff that if they were to organise any function after Isha prayer then it should not last more than ninety minutes. I commend such good practices.

The Prophet's intercession

In these gatherings organised by professional Na'at reciters, professional masters of ceremonies and fake Pirs give the impression that Allah and his Messenger ﷺ are on the side of the sinners whilst the pious and do-gooders have no place. Yet Allah said, *"the most honourable in Allah's sight are the pious and devout".*[60]

The Messenger ﷺ appointed Muaz ibn Jabal as the governor of Yemen. When he dispatched him, Muaz was mounted and the Messenger ﷺ walked alongside him. He offered him this last minute advice. "Perhaps after this year you won't meet me and you will visit my mosque and my grave." Muaz and the others wept when they heard this. Then turning towards Madinah, he said, "the nearest to me are the pious and the devout, whoever they may be and wherever they are".[61]

Some speakers quote the Hadith "my intercession is for my community's major sinners." They embolden the audience by saying, "so we learn that the major sinners will enjoy it there and no one will care about the do-gooders." Allah forbid! This is a subjective and wrong interpretation of the Hadith. The scholars say the Hadith is evidence to refute the dissenters who did not believe that the major sinners deserve intercession.

The experts of Hadith explain: only those who lack faith will be deprived of the intercession, they denied Allah and the Hereafter and will be in hell forever. But

---

[59] Aqaid Al-Nasafi: 8
[60] Al-Hujarat: 13
[61] Ahmed: 22052

those who believed, read the Kalima sincerely and died in the state of faith will receive intercession at some stage, despite being major sinners. So, they won't be deprived of the intercession. You will notice how some public speakers interpret Hadith to please their crowd and to get an applause from them even if it is against the Shariah. Some public speakers use the couplet written by Ala-Hazrat as evidence of their statement:

> *"Wow! how your intercession whets the appetite*
> *so much that it takes away the sinners' burden, so what's piety?"*

This has been taken out of context, Ala-Hazrat meant it for a specific sinner who will get the Messenger's intercession. It is not meant to make Muslims into sinners. The Messenger ﷺ said "I know the last person who will enter Paradise he will be the last to leave hell. This person will be presented before Allah on judgement day. His minor sins would be laid before him but the major sins will be kept hidden. He will be asked about each minor sin and he will admit he did it but he is surprised that no major sin is mentioned. He will be given a merit for every sin; he is now overwhelmed by Divine grace and mercy. So, he accidentally cries out what about my major sins? The Messenger ﷺ smiled; his smile was so broad that we saw his molars.[62]

So, on judgement day there will be some amazing displays of divine mercy that some lucky folks will experience. However, the public speakers ought to prioritise the principles of Shariah rather than the quirky points. The public cannot understand the intricacies and the exceptional cases that are mentioned in the Quran and the Sunnah. It is the scholars' responsibility to encourage people to be pious and avoid sins.

Here is another example: the story of the Israelite who murdered one hundred people and Allah forgave him. So will you tell the story to embolden people to commit murder? Allah forbid! Would you say it doesn't matter so go on killing, eventually you will be forgiven? Or will you explain that this Hadith is an

---

[62] Muslim 5587

example of the limitless mercy of Allah and it is a lesson in never to lose faith in Allah's grace and kindness. Abu Saeed the poet said,

> *"Sinner, stop sinning, whether you are*
> *disbeliever, Zoroastrian or an idolater*
> *return to Allah's grace full of hopeful*
> *you were disloyal hundred times, still come back"*

The Philosopher and poet Iqbal said,

> *"We are gracious but there's no seeker*
> *Who can we show the way, there's no one who seeks destination"*

Speakers should present the principles of Shariah, encourage people to be pious and not to commit minor and major sins. The principle of rhetoric is 'do not interpret a view against its intended purpose'. This applies to these Ahadith, they absolutely condemn the killing of the innocent. The Quran likened the murder of a single person to that of killing an entire humanity. The Messenger ﷺ said, "the murder of an innocent Muslim is more severe than the destruction of the whole world".[63]

To mention the grand intercession of the Messenger ﷺ in a way that makes sins seem trivial will embolden people to sin. It is misleading and will lead to failure in this world and in the Hereafter. Ala-hazrat's couplet explained the perfect nature of the Messenger's grand intercession. The subtleties of religion must not be regarded trivial or petty.

Recommendations for reformation of the conventional religious speeches and gatherings

1) Promote qualified scholars and discourage unqualified public speakers.
2) A melodious voice is Allah's gift however, the priority is to be given to

---

[63] Tirmadhi: 1395

the people of knowledge. Do not give precedence to Na'at recital over scholarly speeches.

3) Instead of preaching from the Quran and Sunnah there are too many unauthentic narrations and even fabricated stories.

4) Scholars must guide and lead the public and not follow their whims and desires.

5) The presentation of good news about Paradise without the warning of sins and their consequences must be avoided.

6) Public speakers who use fabricated narrations in the presence of scholars lower the credibility of qualified scholars.

7) The criticism of wrong practices should not cause conflict in the community.

8) Avoid stretching the gathering late into the night and missing the morning prayer.

9) Shying away from talking about major socio-religious and economic issues is a sign of immaturity.

10) Pay attention to educational institutions and the seeking of religious knowledge by talking about these topics.

11) Stop the promotion of the Master of ceremonies. It is unnecessary.

12) Take care of your neighbourhood: do not blast the loudspeaker to drown other sounds like the music. This is equivalent to 'two wrongs don't make a right.'

13) The recital of Na'at by women on loudspeaker is permissible for women only gatherings.

14) The annual memorial gatherings of the saints (Urs) have turned into an amusement and fanfare that are addressed by professional speakers and promoted by ignorant Pirs.

These are some of the issues that we need to urgently reform.

Chapter 6:
The reformation
of poetry

P oetry is artistic writing which rhymes and is written in verses. It stirs the readers' feelings and imagination with it's effective lyrical arrangement of words and sounds. As an artistic genre of literature, poetry is not forbidden. However, the Shariah will pass judgement on its content. If it is meaningful then, it will be admired, if meaningless or deviant it will be condemned. The Quran has a passage about the poets: *"Shall I tell you who will be visited by the Demons? They will visit every sinful slanderer, who listens readily to them and who is a liar. The deceived poets follow them too. Don't you see them wondering about in every valley, boastfully say things they don't do? Except the believing poets who are righteous, remember Allah a lot and defend themselves against tyranny. The tyrants will soon know the fate they will be returned to".*[64]

The Quran criticised poets for three reasons:
1. They are often confused and fail to distinguish between right and wrong.
2. They say one thing and do another.
3. Sometimes they say unwise things. The Messenger ﷺ distinguished poetry that praises God, his prophets and the saints. He said, "Some Poetry is full of wisdom".[65]

Commentary on the passage about the poets

1. The disbelievers accused the Messenger ﷺ of being a poet so, the Quran responded by rejecting the accusation, "only the misguided follow the poets". This verse praises the disciples of the Messenger ﷺ who are called pious and devout unlike the followers of the poets, who are misguided.
2. Allah said, "Do you not see them wondering about in every valley?" This means they will be found on many stages and different places seeking fame and money. They are condemned because they are unscrupulous and defy the bounds of decency. They have false beliefs

---

[64] Al-Shuara: 221-7
[65] Bukhari: 6145

and compose poetry to satisfy their strange desires. The phrase "Every valley" could refer to all genres of poetry: narrative, lyrical and dramatic.[66] Sometimes they present reality, sometimes they are in the romantic world, using metaphors and metonyms. They are lyrical now and comical in the next moment. Sometimes critiquing and other times praising, now lamenting and now singing odes. They often indulge in absurd and petty topics. Mujahid said "they express things in beautiful words." Qatada said, "Some they flatter others they criticise cruelly".[67]

3. Allah said, "they say what they don't practice." These are poets who don't practice what they say. Imam Baghawi said "Sometimes their poetry is false, making unproven claims and at other times outright lies".[68] Qurtabi explained the verses: "sometimes they turn a coward into a hero and call a miser a generous person likening him to Hatim Tai. They exaggerate the praises of the undeserving. Once the famous poet Farzadiq presented a couplet in the court of Caliph Suleiman ibn Abdal Malik "Drunk women slept with me last night// their virginity I ended." The Caliph was angry with him and handed him a penalty, 'stone him'. So, he quickly responded "doesn't the Quran say, 'they say what they do not practice?" On hearing this he forgave him.[69]

4. When the verses were revealed Hassan, Abdullah Ibn Rawaha and Ka'ab ibn Malik came crying to the Messenger, "Messenger, the Quran has criticised the poets, we are poets." So, Allah revealed "Except the believing poets who are righteous, remember Allah a lot and defend themselves against tyranny." So fair-minded, righteous and scrupulous poets are exempt from this passage. Such poets are commended for their positive qualities. No wonder their poetry is splendid. When the Messenger ﷺ asked Hassan to write poetry ridiculing the Quraish he told him to be accurate and not to exaggerate. He told him to take the advice

---

[66] Baghawi: 3:378
[67] Ibn Jarir: Volume 11:137
[68] Bagawi: 3:278
[69] Qurtabi: Volume 13:134

of Abu Bakr "Abu Bakr is the expert of the Quraish lineage, check it with him and do not write any poetry until you have clarified it with him".[70] Once Ka'ab ibn Zuhair presented a couplet:

"the Messenger ﷺ is a sword from which light spreads everywhere he is the naked sword of India."

The Messenger ﷺ corrected it as follows:

"the Messenger ﷺ is a lamp from which light spreads he is the naked sword of God."

The Messenger ﷺ did not like being called an Indian sword so he changed it to the sword of God.

Writing the Na'at of the Messenger ﷺ is a challenging genre of poetry. Even a slight exaggeration has the danger of idolatry and diminishing the status of the Messenger ﷺ could be disrespectful. That is why the poet must be extremely careful. An unqualified person should not compose a Na'at by themselves. If one is inclined to do so, then make sure it is checked and approved by a qualified scholar. The Messenger ﷺ said, "The good of poetry is amazing whilst the bad is harmful".[71] Knowledgeable and wise poets were praised "a believer strives with his language and with his sword".[72] He said, "some poetry is full of wisdom".[73]

Qadi Sanaullah Panni-Patti wrote "poets who are exempt are the ones who remember a lot so their poetry is also divine remembrance and they remind people of their responsibilities towards Allah's oneness and obedience to him"[74]

Imam Bukhari has a chapter in his book "poetry is disliked if it prevents a

---

[70] Muslim: 2490
[71] Mishkat: 4807
[72] Ahmed: 27052
[73] Bukhari: 6145
[74] Tafsir Mazhari: Volume 5:315

person from the study of the Quran, the Sunnah and the divine remembrance." He cites Hadith "a stomach full of infectious fluid is better than a mind full of wicked poetry".[75]

Examples of poetic and theatrical gaffes

These charlatans have been noted for calling the Angels labourers and Jibril a tailor. This is rudeness since Allah has honoured the Angels and Jibril. "They are honourable servants". Abu Shakoor said, "anyone who shows contempt for the Angels is Kafir".[76] Likewise, to malign the family of the Messenger ﷺ or to compare them with the Messenger ﷺ in such a way that it diminishes the status of the Messenger ﷺ is Kufr. I once saw a banner in a prominent square in the city of Karachi it read:

> "Even Ibrahim couldn't achieve the status of Hussain
> he managed to build the Kaaba but couldn't make the Karbala."

This kind of poetry is condemnable. Ala-Hazrat wrote "reading, listening and writing such poetry is against the Shariah and therefore, forbidden. This includes fabricated stories, vulgar poetry especially if it has contempt for the prophets and the Angels. Some ignorant Na'at poets make serious gaffes that are Kufr."

The Quran frequently mentions delightful scenes of paradise and then invites the reader to seek them. During a battle, a warrior sat down to take a rest. He had a handful of dates and asked the Messenger ﷺ "if I die fighting where will I go?" The Messenger ﷺ replied "Paradise." He put down the dates and jumped on the horse and ran into the battlefield until he was martyred. Here we see that the Messenger ﷺ is urging us to crave for paradise.

In Surat Ale-Imran verse 133 and Al-Hadid verse 21, believers are urged to hurry to paradise. "The Garden of Paradise" is a marked place in the Prophet's

[75] Bukhari: 6154
[76] Al-Tamheed: 112

masjid between his grave and the pulpit. Ala-Hazrat said "The Prophet's shrine and all the mosques will be taken into Paradise."

Therefore, a comparison of Madinah and Paradise in a way that reduces the splendour of paradise is wrong. This is a habit of some poets nowadays. It must stop! Any poetry that shows contempt for paradise whether by word or implication is Kufr. Likewise, poetry that gives the impression of contempt, is wrong. Allama Ibn Abideen said, "any writing whose meaning is impossible to understand- this is sufficient proof for abandoning it - even if there is a possibility of interpretation".[77] The prayer in Masjid al-Haram is multiplied 100,000 times whilst the prayer in Masjid Al-Nabawi is multiplied 10,000 time. Due to his love and passion for Madinah Ala Hazrat said

"okay Madinah is not superior Makkah is great Zahid!
We are lovers, so why are you arguing?"

We don't ignore the Hadith but we recognise the great reward in Makkah. However, to love the inferior is not against the superiority of Makkah. This is a way of expressing the love of the Messenger ﷺ. He did not compare Madinah with paradise instead he yearned to see the beloved ﷺ since that will be a favour of paradise.

Maulana Amjad Azami explained a couplet of Asi, the famous scholarly poet, he wrote "this couplet is not from a sharp-tongued poet who blurts out whatever is in his head but of somebody who understands the Shariah well, therefore we will give him the benefit of the doubt".[78]

Ala-Hazrat was asked to explain the meaning of poetry composed by some unknown and unscrupulous poet. He said, "You should ask me to explain the meanings of a poem composed by some trustworthy and credible poet, not every Tom, Dick and Harry".[79]

---

[77] Radd-ul Mukhtar: Volume 9:482
[78] Fatawa Amjadiya: Volume 4:279
[79] Fatawa Rizwiyya: Volume 29:67

Chapter 7:
The reformation of the Khanagah, the residence of spiritual guide

The residence of the spiritual guide has been a central place of retreat serving the seekers of spirituality. Throughout Islamic history it has been an institution for the promotion of welfare, religious and spiritual development. May Allah keep these beacons of spiritual guidance forever. Unfortunately, we have noticed certain poor practices sneaking into these places, so they need urgent reform.

1. Some retreats no longer provide appropriate teachings of their orders. Instead they are unproductive places. How can Qadri Sufi criticise the disciples? Not possible, since the books of the father of Qadri spiritual order Shaykh Abdul Qadir Jilani presented clearly the beliefs of Ahl As-Sunnah Wal-Jamaah in his books: Fath-ur Rabbani; Futhuhul Ghayb and Sirrul Asrar. Likewise, the Kashaf al-Mahjub of Ali Hujwari. These classics of Islamic spiritual teachings explain the respect of disciples including that of Amir Muawiya. He said "may Allah humiliate Yazid but not his father".[80]

The spiritual order of Naqashband has similar gems: for example the letters of Mujadad Alif-sani Shaykh Ahmed Sirhindi, anyone who studies these letters cannot sympathise with the Rafadites or the dissenters. The same applies to the Chishti order, the followers have the Treasury of wisdom of 'Saba' Sanabal'; 'Fawaid al-Fawad'; the Malfuzat of Khwaja Taunsi'. They have rich material which protects the readers from the extremes of the deviant sects.

When a follower of Sultan Bahu reads 'Aqle-Bidar' or 'Nur al-Huda' - which explain the greatness of the four Caliphs – he cannot be influenced by the Rafadites or the dissenters. He wrote "I have nothing to do with the Rafadites and the dissenters, I am a Sunni, lover of the four Caliphs, whoever wants to see the beloved Messenger ﷺ, his disciples and the five pure souls his heart will blossom like a flower." He drew a diagram with the name of the Caliphs, Hassan, Hussain, Fatima and Shaykh Abdul

---

[80] Kashaf-al Mahjub: 78

Qadir Jilani. Underneath he wrote "anyone who has Shaykh Abdul Qadir Jilani in mind and keeps this diagram in front of him will be blessed with a vision of the beloved Messenger ﷺ and Caliphs".[81]

The Suhrawardy order has the classic 'Awaref al-Muarif', so their Sufis can receive authentic teachings of Ahl As-Sunnah Wal-Jamaah. Jami Hindi wrote two couplets:

My school is Hanafi, my religion Ibrahimi
I am dust of Ghaus-e-Azam, living in the shade of Saints

2. The representatives and directors of the retreat must provide religious education and opportunities for spiritual development. The children of the spiritual guide must be qualified in Shariah, so they are true heirs of their father. They must not occupy this significant seat of spirituality and moral wisdom just because they happen to be the children of the spiritual guide but because they are fit for it. This will prevent bad practices and innovations creeping into these retreats.

3. Unfortunately, in some places there is no system of education for the seekers who visit them. This is a missed opportunity to reform and help the public. The annual commemoration service, the Urs has changed into mere amusement and fanfare. They wish to keep their ignorant followers by hook or by crook so, they spread superstitions and weird innovations. At one time the retreat could be described as:

Wonderful is the masjid and the retreat
ringing nonstop with the teachings of the beloved Messenger ﷺ

4. Our society can be deceptive sometimes so, the Sufi regretfully says, "in the past Sufism wasn't a name but reality but today it is a name without a reality." This is because some impostors have adopted the garb of the Shaykh and made it a business. Recently in Sargodha in Pakistan a false shaykh killed 20 innocent people.

---

[81] Aqle-Bidar: 208

The conditions for becoming a spiritual guide

Ala-Hazrat said, the guide is of two kinds:

a) General guide refers to the speech of Allah, the Majestic Quran; the Sunnah of the Messenger, the teachings of the imams of Shariah and Tariqah and the scholars. The order is: the public is guided by the scholar; the scholar is guided by the teachings of the imams; the imams are guided by the teachings of the Messenger; and the Messenger ﷺ receives the Divine speech of Allah. A spiritual guide who is empty of religious education is a useless impostor.

b) Special guide, this refers to the oath of allegiance one takes at the hand of a scholar who has the correct Sunni beliefs and who is authorised by the spiritual guide to take oaths. This is a special guide variously known as a Murshid, Shaykh or Pir. The special guide is of two kinds:

The first type: Shaykh Itisal:
By taking the oath of allegiance the seeker is linked with the Messenger ﷺ, there are four conditions to become Shaykh Itisal. They are:

1. The chain of spiritual guides must be intact and connect with the Messenger ﷺ without breaking. In other words, it is a continuous unbroken chain of spiritual guides linked together. Some wrongly think that they can inherit the mantle of a spiritual guide without taking the oath of allegiance. Others are part of a chain that has been severed. Anyone who takes the oath of allegiance in such an order is considered to be invalid. This is like milking an ox or wanting a child from a barren wife. Both are irrational.

2. The spiritual guide must have the correct Sunni beliefs. Someone outside the fold of Ahl As-Sunnah Wal-Jamaah will be misled and mislead

others and will not lead to the Messenger ﷺ. Some irreligious and misguided people have also taken this honourable title of the Pir. Ironically some Wahhabis have jumped on the bandwagon to catch naive people in their snares, so be advised! "Satan's have assumed the human form, so don't give your seeker's hand into any hand."

3. The spiritual guide must be a scholar, know beliefs, Fiqh, be able to distinguish between Kufr and Islam, guidance and misguidance. Otherwise if he isn't misguided today, he will be misguided tomorrow. "The one who does not know evil is likely to fall into it." There are hundreds of statements and gestures that can easily mislead an ignorant person accidentally. When such a person is given an honourable title, it goes to his head and he will reject the advice of the scholars. *"When he is told to be mindful of Allah, pride drives him to sin, his outcome is bad"* (Baqarah: 206). Even if he accepts the advice and repents by refreshing his faith, he does it by himself, failing to get his disciples to do the same. He doesn't realise that his oath of allegiance has been nullified therefore it must be renewed and his disciples' must renew their oath too. Nor does he suspend his activities as the Shaykh but he continues to direct and initiate new disciples with a broken chain. To avoid these problems, the Shaykh must be a scholar.

4. The Shaykh must be free of major sins, a devout person who performs all the obligatory, recommended and the voluntary duties of the Shariah. He must avoid offensive and disliked activities. Though the oath of allegiance is not nullified by committing a major sin, to request a Fasiq to be a Shaykh is tantamount to honouring the person who is disreputable in Shariah.

The second type: Shaykh Isale:
This type of spiritual guide is someone who satisfies the four conditions mentioned above and is proficient at teaching and reforming others.

He has a strong character and leads his followers by good example. When he sees anyone of his followers indulging in evil, he will correct and reform him. He is neither 'a seeker' nor someone 'absorbed'. Both would render him unfit for this office. A seeker is a novice and lacks knowledge and expertise to guide others whilst 'the absorbed' (Majzub) is not sober therefore he is unfit to guide others.

The oath of allegiance also known as Bait. It is of two types: Bait of blessings or bait of compliance and devotion Iradat.

1. Bait of blessing: many people nowadays take this oath of allegiance. There is nothing wrong with this if it is sought sincerely and not for worldly gains. The oath of blessings is beneficial since it registers one among the chain of devout and righteous people that leads to the Messenger ﷺ and finally to Allah.[82]

2. Bait of compliance and devotion (Iradat): the seeker genuinely seeks guidance and is looking for someone who can help him to live morally and spiritually so he can attain divine closeness. He regards the Pir as his teacher, director and leader so, obeys him and does not do anything without his permission, whether he fully grasps the Shaykh's instructions or not he follows them meticulously. This is like Moses who followed Khidr (The mystical green man mentioned in the Quran). Khidr the Shaykh did not allow Moses to ask questions. One just follows the Shaykh, like a corpse in the hands of the funeral director. This is the true oath of allegiance that takes one to Allah. This is the oath the Messenger ﷺ took from his disciples. Ubaid ibn Samat said, "we took the oath of the Messenger ﷺ to obey him in ease and difficulty, in happiness and sadness and not to doubt him".[83]

Note: Ala-Hazrat's opinion is about the spiritual guide who is a scholar and able to distinguish between right and wrong and practices of Shariah and Tariqah

---

[82] Fatawa Rizwiyya: Volume 21:505
[83] Fatawa Rizwiyya: Volume 21:509

secondary. He excludes the imposters with insincere intentions who wear the mantle of the righteous masters. They mislead people, have mixed gatherings and commit evils. Sadly, we have many examples from the recent past.

Innovations and bad practices at the holy shrines

Unfortunately, some shrines have become the centres of poor practices and innovations including selling and buying of drugs. We must purify these holy places of such bad practices. I visited the shrine of the famous Saint Shahbaz Qalandar in Sindh and gave a press conference there. I said, "there is no room for the mixing of men and women and the practice of dancing in the Shariah. Because of this culture, drug addicts and other criminals come here. This culture has no relationship with Sufism nor with the spirituality, self-purification, moral development and the teachings of Ihsan and gnosis. This culture is the opposite to all these wonderful Islamic practices. Scholars specify that women should not attend shrines. I can now understand why, precisely for this reason. The purpose of the Ministry of religious affairs is to preserve these holy shrines and protect them from corrupt practices. It seems that the ministry has failed to carry out it's responsibility. I have noticed that imams appointed by the Ministry do not lead the prayers as they ought to consequently, residents employ their own imams in the masjids. Similarly, the masjids are not maintained nor decorated by the ministry so, the people raise their own funds and run them. The question is what is the ministry doing?"

There is an urgent need to reform the management and upkeep of the holy shrines and their masjids. We recommend that the ministry sets up a board of senior scholars and spiritual guides to oversee the running and the functioning of these holy sites. The corrupt and unscrupulous caretakers that are appointed at these holy shrines should be dismissed and replaced by competent scholars, capable of the management of the holy site. Iqbal the poet and philosopher of

Pakistan criticised the charlatans at these holy shrines:

They've inherited the mantle of guidance
the falcon's nest is in the clutches of vultures
The guides who sell and gorge
Abu Zarr's blanket, Awais's cloak and Fatima's scarf

Chapter 8:
The reformation of the Ramadan broadcasts on TV channels

Since the independent TV channels came on the media scene, we have seen a new trend during the month of Ramadan. Most TV channels broadcast sacrilegious programmes under the banner of Ramadan. This is like putting a 'pure water' label on a bottle of wine. I am not objecting to the scholars appearing on these TV channels to teach. That is good, I am speaking about the scholars who take part in programmes that exploit the vulnerable, have un-Islamic practices and violate the sanctity of Ramadan. I do not blame the scholars for these bad practices. I support any TV channel that preserves Islamic practices. Last year I wrote a column for a national newspaper titled 'the cry of Ramadan.'

The cry of Ramadan

Since the inception of independent TV channels, no one has assessed their benefit and harm to the Pakistani society. One clear benefit of independent TV channels has been to tackle corruption, consequently the politicians are fearful of it. So, corruption can no longer be kept secret. On the other hand, the media has sensationalised political and social issues to such an extent that they are no longer assessed objectively. You hardly see an objective discussion based on arguments and proofs. Instead there is a lot of noise. An aggressive style seems to be preferred over calm and unruffled discussion. There is more noise of the waterfall than the calm of the sea and the voice of rationality is far less common. The reason? Ratings or public viewing figures. The viewership determines the rate of marketing. I believe that Pakistani society has paid a heavy price with the loss of moral, social and spiritual values. It is too big a price.

Another major casualty has been the violation of the sanctity of the holy month of Ramadan. During Ramadan people turn more religious and there is a heightened sense of devotion as people wish to benefit from the blessings of this month. The benefits and the blessings of this month acquire a special dimension. The Messenger ﷺ said "when Ramadan arrives the gates of paradise are flung open, none remain closed. The doors of hell are closed and none remain open. The rebellious Satan is chained and tied up."

The atmosphere of Ramadan motivates righteous deeds and inhibits evil. The media markets Ramadan with songs, slogans and creates a fanfare around its various themes: rewards of Ramadan; guests of Ramadan; splendour of Ramadan, faith of Ramadan and all other weird and wonderful topics. Someone frustrated by these exploitations remarked "it would be better if all of them took the title "the shop of Ramadan." It is this "shop of Ramadan" scene that is all over the media with actresses leading the way to Paradise. Can someone justify this from the Quran?

Ramadan is a time of spirituality and devotion. When you have mixed gathering of men and women, it is more like a concert or a marketplace and nobody cares about the time of the prayer, in fact, prayer is discouraged. Fanfare and showbiz are spiced with religious sentiments and phrases and sprinkled with religious chutney, the rest is pure marketing. Can the gurus of Harvard University MBA marketing course compete with this? These marketing experts use the religious labels with expertise to sell advertisements. Somebody told me about a Ramadan marketing meeting at a major TV channel in which they were told, all the spots for the Azans in Lahore have been sold but the contract for Karachi is pending. A sad story, Azan has been commoditised like sugar and flour. The Quran speaks *"Stay away from those who regard their religion as a sport, amusement and are deceived by the attractions of this worldly life. To prevent any person being needlessly lost to hell because of the fruits of their actions, they will have no protector or intercessor beside Allah, nor will any ransom be accepted. They will be in hell as a result of their actions; they denied so they shall have boiling water and painful punishment."*[84]

"The people who made their religion fanfare, a sport and were deceived by worldly life. Today we shall abandon them just as they neglected their meeting with us on this day, they disputed our signs."[85]

---

[84] Al-Anam: 70
[85] Al-Araf: 51

Today Ramadan is lamenting, crying out that its sanctity has been ruined, 'Jafa par wafa' in the words of Dr Iqbal, 'it's being loyal despite the betrayal.' The Holiness of Ramadan is cleverly wrapped up in colourful wretchedness and evil. The name 'Islam' raises holy and pure thoughts in the listeners but, it is at the mercy of artists and the flickering of neon lights. The artist should not don the robe of holiness, please wear your real colours! There are plenty of opportunities to express your artistic talent. Those who want to do drama or comedy can do so but wearing Islam's robe is 'Jafa par wafa' and totally unnecessary. A Juristic principle or a proverb may be specific, but the rule applies to everyone. Sahar Ludhyani captured it in this couplet:

> Where are they, where are they? The preservers of self-respect
> where are they? The fans of holiness of the East?

Were we to change the phrase 'holiness of the East' to 'holiness of the religion' the message becomes clearer. It is unfortunate that industrialists and big businessmen go to Hajj and Umrah without a break every year. Why don't they sponsor religious programmes? Furthermore, women dressed inappropriately are presenters and anchors of these Ramadan broadcasts. This is playing with religion and is duplicity. Something we used to see in films, where, in one scene the actor is a thief and in the next he is sitting on the prayer mat with a rosary. The questioner asks, 'how ironic?' He answers, "that's my job, this is my religion." The message is, anything goes with religion so people are blatantly exploiting Islam.

There are large religious organisations and Islamic political parties who are not concerned with this at all. If anybody makes a slight mistake, they kick up a fuss, but the disrespect of the holy month goes unnoticed. People have given up and accepted defeat. Is this because the media is so powerful and intimidating? Or have we compromised with it? This is a serious matter that needs to be addressed with the media moguls. We need to educate and raise their awareness and understanding. So, they can restore the honour of Ramadan. In the Seerah conference of 2012, I made a recommendation to the president of the Islamic

Republic of Pakistan, Mamnoon Hussain, I suggested that rather than being satisfied with fiery speeches, let us be practical and engage the media moguls. This requires the setting up of a committee of experts, a vigilance cell that would monitor the media's output with regards to moral social and spiritual values. I cannot think of any media mogul who would not co-operate. We need to be encouraging them to purge the media of wretchedness and evil. Nobody is willing to take this responsibility, seriously.

Someone said "the brave and the determined are absent, so are the seekers of exemption. Consequently there is no one to stand up for the dignity of religion. Therefore, calmness is reported everywhere. But anyone determined to tackle the issue would be regarded as rigid, backward and failing to understand the needs of the time and doesn't have his finger on the pulse."

Perhaps Ghalib the 19th century Urdu poet had this in mind when he wrote:

> They are people of the past don't say anything to them
> they regard wine and songs patrons of pleasure

The chairman of the Pakistan Ministry of Religious Affairs, was active in ensuring that the funeral of Mumtaz Qadri was not broadcast on the media. Will he take steps to protect the sanctity of the Quran and the month of Ramadan? Last year half a dozen writers drew our attention to this matter and I ask them to pick up their pens and do the same again, this Ramadan. Regard it as Zakat you pay for the gift of writing that Allah has given you. It is frequently heard that religious people just cry on social media and do nothing.

Chapter 9:
The reformation of the farewell Friday in Ramadan

The Messenger ﷺ picked Friday as 'the best of all days.' It is a holy day of Islam and as such all Fridays are equal in their sacredness. However, the Hadith states any obligatory duty performed in Ramadan earns seventy times more reward, so the Fridays of Ramadan are special. The Messenger ﷺ said, "whoever performs an obligatory duty in Ramadan he will get the reward of seventy times." Considering this prophetic saying, the value of Friday prayer in the congregation is also multiplied seventy times. However, all the Fridays are equal. There is no evidence of the final Friday of Ramadan as being special. There is neither a saying of the Messenger ﷺ or the Caliphs or the imams.

But we have noticed this new trend where special attention is paid to the final Friday of Ramadan. Na'at reciters mourn the departure of the month to create a sombre mood. There is no evidence for this. I wrote a Fatwa for a national paper, here I present some excerpts from it:

Shariah ruling on the last Friday of Ramadan

In some places people call the last Friday of Ramadan 'Jumma al-Wida', and in the sermon include the words "farewell, farewell O month of Ramadan!". The Na'at reciters lament. There is no evidence from the Messenger ﷺ for such activity. Ala-Hazrat was asked:

1. Did the Messenger ﷺ read the last sermon in Ramadan?
2. If he did not, then who invented it?
3. What is the status of the last Friday sermon? Is it obligatory, necessary, recommended, preferable or permissible?
4. The one who misses it, is he a sinner?

He answered:
1. There is no proof for the last Friday sermon in Hadith
2. It is not established from the disciples and we do not know the innovator.
3. It is permissible if there are not other factors, which make it

reprehensible or forbidden.

4. The sermon on Friday is a condition of Friday prayer but, the so-called 'final sermon' is not. Ignoring it has no impact on the Friday prayers validity.[86]

In this Fatwa Ala-Hazrat cited a quotation from 'Shabeh-al-insan': "to recite the phrases of lament on the final Friday of Ramadan is permissible, although there is no evidence from the venerable teachers. It is best not to do it, lest the public think it is obligatory or the practice of the Messenger ﷺ. It should not be falsely attributed to the Messenger ﷺ as someone claimed, "Allah's beloved Messenger ﷺ used to express his sorrow at the departure of Ramadan by saying 'O month of Ramadan farewell." Ala-Hazrat said "I agree with everything said in this Fatwa except "it is best not done". This should be changed to "it should not be done regularly ans sometimes it can be left out so that the public can know it is not necessary or recommended. Scholars recommend that when something is left out it sends the signal that it is not necessary."

Someone asked him "is saying farewell, farewell permissible?" He said "there is no ruling about this farewell and it is not prohibited however, the scholars should not make it a regular feature of their Ramadan. The true farewell is from the heart when you feel the departure of this month otherwise it is a matter of show"[87]

Clarification of a fake report

In the time of Ala-Hazrat, some preachers would say farewell in their Friday sermon. However, nowadays we have Na'at reciters who sing in sombre tones till people are touched and made to cry. They quote a book by the name of 'Anees al-Wa'ezeen' which says, "whoever rejoices at the coming of Ramadan and laments at it's departure will enter Paradise, it is on Allah to admit him into paradise." There are other fabricated reports in this book too. Despite doing

---

[86] Fatawa Rizwiyya: Volume 8:451
[87] Fatawa Rizwiyya: Volume 8:451-454

a thorough research for this narration in the books of Hadith, we were not able to find it. In his response Ala-Hazrat said "to say farewell on the final Friday of Ramadan is permissible as long as it is not attributed to the Messenger ﷺ. Lay people are not aware that the basis on which they say the farewell is as we have shown, fake and to believe it as truth is wrong."

"The truth is if the final sermon of farewell is couched in subtle language then there is nothing against it. The best practice is to follow the way of the Messenger ﷺ and the disciples. It is the best way to stop an innovation being perceived necessary by the public. So, people do not regard it as the Sunnah of the Messenger ﷺ."

Scholars should not indulge in activities that lead people to think of it as a Sunnah of the Messenger ﷺ. The jurists have stopped the reading of Surat al-Dahr and Al-Sajda in the morning prayer on Friday, yet this is proven from well-known reports. Similarly, the jurists have stopped the performance of a prostration after the witr prayer. There are many examples of this kind where there is a danger of the permissible act being perceived as Sunnah leading to Bidah. The farewell sermon is so well established in our region that the public think it is according to Sunnah. The scholars should stop this. This is my opinion, others might have a different opinion.

Therefore, it is the duty of the scholars to educate the public about this situation and to clarify to them that by shedding a few tears does not make you, the heir of paradise. There is permissibility of saying the farewell however, we should not insist on announcing it. If someone is sad at the departure of the month of Ramadan, that is wonderful and it is the sign of a healthy heart. You do not need Na'at reciters to move your heart.

The purpose of the devotions of Ramadan is to make worship a permanent feature of our lives throughout the year. However, if someone wants to make this prayer "Lord of the universe, give us these blessings again and again." This is a wonderful prayer for longevity and it is according to the Sunnah.

Chapter 10:
The reformation of
the Friday sermon

I n his Friday sermons the blessed Messenger ﷺ taught the recently revealed verses of the Quran or discussed new expeditions and campaigns. The Caliphs in their sermons did the same and addressed the public to make them aware of their programmes and campaigns. The sermon is like 'the state of the union address' of the President of America. The purpose of the Friday sermon is to inspire and educate Muslims to be devout. It is an opportunity to reform and spread the teachings of Islam.

The Sunnah is the Arabic sermon, as in the time of the Messenger ﷺ and continues till today. But not everybody understands Arabic so, there is a speech in the native language before the short Arabic sermon. The sermon is to teach Islam and instil the love of Islamic values. By talking about daily activities, we can show how they relate to Islamic teachings. The challenge is to show they are relevant then, people will listen to them. Particularly the young people who want to see Islamic solutions to their problems. A good style of sermon is to sow the seeds of good ideas rather than imposing duties on people. This is best achieved through storytelling, instead of providing raw and dry logical evidence. The Quran said, *"invite to the way of your Lord with wisdom and effective teachings and discuss politely"*.[88]

---

[88] Al-Nahl: 125

Chapter 11:
The reformation
of repentance

There are many religious practices that we perform but they are empty of spiritual reality. They are mere skeletons of rituals. Over the past years, television channels have started to broadcast religious gatherings in which Na'at reciters chant "may Allah accept my repentance". People think by listening to or saying these words they have repented. Repentance is not chanting such phrases melodiously but rather it is spiritual devotion coming from the depths of the heart. There are five conditions for repentance:

1. A sincere acknowledgement of the sin

2. A sense of shame for committing the sin. The Messenger ﷺ said "Shame is repentance".[89]

3. Compensation of the victim of the sin. Anyone mistreated or deprived of their right, must be compensated:
   - Missed obligatory prayers, they must be made up one by one
   - The unpaid zakat must be paid for all the missed years
   - The missed fasts of Ramadan can be atoned by fasting
   - If anyone was hurt or deprived of their right they must be compensated

4. Pledge never to repeat the sin and seek Allah's help for fulfilment of the pledge.

5. Sin committed in public must be repented publicly.

Muaz asked the Messenger ﷺ "Messenger, give me advice, he said 'be mindful of Allah as much as you can, remember him plenty where ever you are and if you do something wrong then seek Allah's forgiveness, if it is in secret do so secretly and if it is done openly seek repentance openly".[90]

Can the supplication be chanted melodiously?

Ala-Hazrat's father Maulana Naqi Ali Khan wrote: "the manners of supplication, du'a, manners of rhyming and humming should be avoided when making supplication as it takes away sincerity. The Hadith mentions "do not

---

[89] Sunan ibn Majah: 4252
[90] Tabarani Muajam ul Kabir: 331

use rhymes in supplication".[91] Ala-Hazrat said "the prophetic prayers did not add artificial rhyming they are comprehensive prayers that rhyme naturally." In supplication there should not be any humming and melody. This is against the manners of supplication. The best way to supplicate is to use the prayers of the beloved Messenger ﷺ. These are found in the books of Hadith and they cover all our needs.

Ala-Hazrat cited Ibn Ameer al-Haj Halbi "humming in the prayer is not permissible. This manner of supplication is not allowed since it sounds playful. From experience we know a beggar would not sing his request like an entertainer before the King as that would be considered disrespectful. Supplication is a time to be humble and solemn".[92]

Considering these rules, the pious believer will return to Allah in repentance quietly and earnestly seeking the Lord's forgiveness. However, if the sin was committed openly the repentance must be declared in open forum. Each sin must be separately repented, one by one. For specific sins one must make specific repentance, general repentance is not valid.

How to atone for missed prayers

There is a baseless report that says "one can have his life's missed prayers atoned for by praying four units of voluntary prayer on special nights. So, hundreds and thousands of missed prayers can be atoned by praying just four units. He will not be punished." This is a false report, misleading and an innovation. We do not know who found this shortcut. After becoming 'responsible' every Muslim must pray five times a day. They are accountable and answerable for each prayer and any prayer that is missed must be made up. Someone asked Ala-Hazrat "People say that by praying four units of voluntary prayer on the last Friday of Ramadan, the whole life's missed prayers can be atoned for." He replied, "this is an innovation, a Bidah and has no basis from any credible book." [93]

---

[91] Ihya ulum udeen: Volume 2:405
[92] Fatawa Rizwiyya: Volume 28:165
[93] Fatawa Rizwiyya: Volume 7:417

On another occasion someone asked "on the last Friday of Ramadan some people pray in congregation and the prayer is as a compensation for their missed prayers. Is this permissible? He replied "people have invented this way of atoning for their missed prayers, it is an evil innovation and the narration about it is fabricated. This is strictly forbidden and is misguidance. The Messenger ﷺ said "anyone who misses the obligatory prayer and then remembers it must pray. There is no other way of atoning for it. Abu Qatada presented as an evidence the verse "and pray regularly to remember me".[94] Allama Mullah Ali Qari said "the Hadith which people cite about the missed prayers, 'whoever prayed four units on the last Friday of Ramadan his seventy of missed prayers would be atoned for." He said "this is false and there is a consensus that nothing can substitute for prayers that were missed except by praying each one of them."

Imam Ibn Hajr Makki and Allama Zarqani wrote "there is a worse innovation in some towns. On Friday they offer five prayers with the intention that any prayers they missed that year or in the past would be atoned for. This is not true for several reasons and in fact it is forbidden".[95] Allama Ghulam Rasul Saeedi wrote "we learn from this Hadith that a person who misses his prayer because of sleep or carelessness must make up for it".[96] Anyone who practices this way of atoning for missed prayer is mistaken. It may be likened to the person who gives three divorces to his wife and the Imam tells him to give charity to the needy to revoke the divorce and return to his wife. This is false and not allowed as it is violating the Shariah. May Allah protect us from such innovations.

In our writings we often condemn people who do not practice the Shariah. We called them imposters. We also condemn the spiritual guides who innovate and do not follow the Ahl As-Sunnah Wal-Jamaah.

---

[94] Muslim: 684
[95] Sharh Zarqani Volume 7:110
[96] Tibyan al-Quran: 7:355

By condemning such imposters, we are promoting the true scholars of religion and the rightful heirs of the spiritual guides. When we condemn the ignorant preachers, we are promoting the righteous and genuine preachers. I hope people will not misunderstand our reformation and criticism of the people of innovation.

"Lord! Show us the truth as it is and give us the ability to follow it; show us the evil as it is and give us the ability to avoid it. Ameen, O Lord of the universe! Bless us through our beloved master Muhammad ﷺ."

Appendix 1:
Ala-Hazrat
Maulana Ahmed
Raza Khan Qadri

The Reviver of the Islamic Spirit

Dr Musharraf Hussain first published this biography in 1978 from the Islamic Society of Aston University, Birmingham, where he was the president of the Islamic Society.

It is no small task to introduce a personality regarded as the symbol of the traditional and orthodox interpretation of Islam:
Ala-Hazrat Khan Qadri (Ala-Hazrat). He is famous for his scholarly interpretation of the Quran, the Prophetic Sunnah and the Sufi practices. He represented the Ahl As-Sunnah Wal-Jamaah in the 1880's and was concerned about the Islamic spirit which was being corrupted in the Indian sub-continent by the plots of the British Raj and the extremism of the rising cults in the region. Ala-Hazrat was the leading light of this "Islamic revival" and was a dynamic individual. Fondly known as Ala'Hazrat. The title "Ala'Hazrat" means "great person" and is a fitting title for the Imam, who was a Scholar, Mufti, a Mufassir and a Muhaddith. This polymath was a man of Allah, with a deep and vast breadth of knowledge in all the religious sciences. The love for The Prophet Muhammad ﷺ and his Sunnah underpinned the Imam's teachings and reformative activities. The term "Barelivi" is often used to refer to his admirers, who promote his thought and teachings.

Early Life

Born in 1856, Ala-Hazrat came of a reputed family of theologians of Bareilly in India. His father Imam Naqi Ali Khan was a scholar and author of several books and likewise his grandfather Imam Raza Ali Khan was a renowned scholar and a Sufi. The great forefathers of Ala-Hazrat migrated from Qandahar during the Mogul rule and settled in Lahore.

Ala-Hazrat studied Islamic sciences from his father and undertook the traditional Darse-Nizami course. This was the time when the Muslim rule over India had ended and the British Raj had begun. Many Muslim scholars and leaders were executed or imprisoned for life by the British. The young Maulana must have heard about the British savagery of the innocent Muslims as well as their conspiracies to weaken the Muslims. Furthermore, the British sponsored and encouraged new heretical movements which undermined the unity of the Muslims. His father instilled the love of the blessed Prophet Muhammad ﷺ, so much so that he believed that if the Muslims continue to love him, they would never lose.

Maulana was an industrious student, with his strong retentive memory and razor-sharp wit he completed the study of the formative Islamic sciences at fourteen. He was excellent in the study of Arabic literature, grammar, syntax and lexicology. His proficiency in this field proved immensely beneficial to him later in the composition of his own works. The titles of hundreds of his monographs, books and treatise are in Arabic. He was a proficient poet who composed poetry in Arabic and his mastery over Urdu poetry is now well established too. His anthology, "Hadaiq-e-Bakhshish" (Gardens of magnanimity), is the first of its kind devoted solely to the praise of the blessed Prophet Muhammad ﷺ.

Al-Hazrat took the oath of allegiance to Hazrat Sayyid Ally-Rasool of Marahra, who was a devout Sufi and a saint of his time. The oath is a pledge which implies a determination to turn away from sin and to pattern one's life in accordance with Allah's way under the guidance of the spiritual teacher.

Ala-Hazrat's mentor immediately gave him the mantle of deputy and granted him a certificate for teaching Hadith to others. Seeing this extraordinary event, an older disciple quipped "Master! You only confer the robe of deputy on someone who has undergone a long devotional exercise." Sayyid Ally-Rasool replied, "Other people come to me with an impure heart and their purification takes time but, Ala-Hazrat came with an illuminated soul. For a long time I have been worried but, by Allah's grace it is over today, in the Hereafter when Allah asks me, Ally-Rasool what have you brought with you? Then I shall present my Ala-Hazrat."

In 1878, Ala-Hazrat travelled to Haramain-Sharifain for the Hajj in the company of his father. Here he met many scholars, notably Mufti Ahmad Dahlan ash-Shafie and Mufti Abdul Rahman al-Hanafi. The Doctors of Theology granted him certificates in Hadith, Fiqh, exegesis, etc… This must have been a wonderful occasion for the young scholar to be honoured by the dignitaries of Makkah and Madinah.

A Strategy for Economic Recovery

For the political and the socio-religious revival of the Muslims, Ala-Hazrat stressed the importance of economic well-being. In his book, "A strategy for reformation and success" he proposed a four-point strategy for the economic recovery of Muslims. The book is a clear testimony of his anxiety for the salvation of Muslims. His proposed strategy was as follows:

1. The Muslims should solve all their disputes amongst themselves and thus save the enormous legal costs.
2. The wealthy Muslims of Bombay, Calcutta, Rangoon, Madras and Hyderabad should open their own banks.
3. The Muslims should only buy from Muslims.
4. Everyone should strive to preserve and spread the message of Islam.

Encyclopaedic Knowledge

Ala-Hazrat occupied a high rank among his contemporary scholars, who acknowledged his mastery over Islamic learning, exegesis, traditions, jurisprudence, Arabic grammar and syntax, and doctrinal theology. He utilised this encyclopaedic knowledge in his career of intellectual and literary pursuits. A conspicuous feature of his writings is that they are written in a forceful style, maybe because many of them were written in the defence of orthodox Islamic teachings. Even the fundamental basic beliefs were being challenged by ever growing movements of Sir Sayyid Ahmad Khan, the revolt of the Qadiyani's and the newly imported "Wahhabi" movement. All of these posed a real threat to the Orthodox and balanced teachings of Islam.

Ala-Hazrat wrote in defence, with a superb authoritative and a forceful style, of the Islamic creed, numerous books including "Introduction to beliefs", "The sword of Haramain", "Pure Beliefs" and "Splendour of belief". And for the moral, social and spiritual reformation, the "Rizvian Judicial Verdicts" is his masterpiece. This is a compilation of his Fatwas on every conceivable aspect of life, consisting of thirty volumes and spread over some 30,000 pages. Ala-Hazrat possessed a photographic memory and a radiant flame of intellect. Whatever he read or heard was treasured in his memory.

Following the Sunnah

Ala-Hazrat had a great love for the blessed Prophet ﷺ. When anyone returned from the Hajj, he would ask if they had visited the blessed Prophet's ﷺ masjid and he would then kiss their hands with respect. In his last days, he wrote a letter to an Imam, "My journey is drawing to its end, I do not want to die in India nor in Makkah, but in Madinah and buried in Baqi." Maulana Ahmad Raza expressed his love for the blessed Prophet ﷺ through his poetry:

> The sincere heart is imbued with your memory
> the head forgone at your feet
> Heart, soul, mind and intellect have arrived in Madinah
> are you not going Raza when all has gone?

However, Ala-Hazrat rejected the idea of love without obedience to the beloved Prophet ﷺ. He tried to follow the Sunnah to its minutest detail and encouraged others to do the same. He was very strict about performing the prayers with congregation and even when he was ill, he would walk to the masjid. He wore the turban during the prayers, the head dress of the beloved Prophet ﷺ. His prayers were illustrations of complete submission, total devotion and sincerity.

Ala-Hazrat died at the age of 65 on the 25th of Safr 1340AH (1921 AD) on Friday at the time when the muezzin was saying "come to success". Just before his death, he gave the following advice: "Keep reciting Surah Yasin, Surah Ra'd and Darud-Sharif until I am breathing. At the last gasp, give me cold water and recite the Kalima … and when my breathing stops close my eyes and straighten my hands and feet. Do not mourn. Carry out the ghusl and shrouding according to the Sunnah."

Glossary

Aqaid, Plural of Aqeeda, belief. It is what we accept as the truth. The Islamic creed is the set of beliefs, they are succinctly summarised in 'Aqaid al Nasafi' written in the eleventh century. Available from www.karimia.com

Ba'it, oath of allegiance taken on the hands of an authorised spiritual guide for personal development and spiritual enlightenment

Bidah, innovation, introduction of a new practice into Shariah that has no precedence. This can be a good innovation or a bad innovation: a good innovation is something that is not forbidden in the Shariah and supports and strengthens the performance of religious duties, whilst bad Bidah is wrong and against the spirit/word of the Shariah.

Fardh, obligatory, category of ruling that must be practised, its negligence is sinful, and denial leads to Kufr.

Fasiq, the sinner, someone who commits major sins thereby violates the Shariah. Some of the major sins are adultery, lying and cheating, murder, stealing, disobedience of parents.

Haram, forbidden category of ruling that must be avoided, leads to major sin and its denial is Kufr.

Hukm, a legal ruling that can be any of the categories of Fardh, wajib, Sunnah, mustahab, haram or makruh.

Ijma, the consensus of the early Imams of the first two centuries (645-850 CE).

Iradat, (literally seeking someone) technically admiration, obedience and loyalty to a spiritual guide.

Khawarij, the dissenters, originally this was the group that opposed Ali and refused to accept his caliphate.

Makruh, offensive anything that is disliked by the Shariah, it must be avoided however it is not sin and its denial is not Kufr.

Milad, the birthday celebrations of the blessed Messenger on the twelfth of Rabiulawwal.

Mizmar, Oboe, a wind instrument used in Qawwali, the devotional singing.

Muhkam, definitive or determined, used for the text that is clear, with fixed meanings that are well understood, there is no ambiguity.

Mutashabihat, ambiguous, metaphorical term used to describe text that has more than one meaning and is open to interpretation.

Mustahab, the preferred, category of ruling that is liked in the Shariah and its abandoning is not sinful.

Na'at, genre of poetry in which the Messenger is praised, his qualities and spiritual beauty eulogised fervently.

Nifaq, hypocrisy, double faced, duality in faith and action so, the principle and practice don't match, hiding one's inner reality and conviction.

Qawwali, the devotional singing in the Indian subcontinent often with musical instruments, oboe, guitar tambourine and small drums.

Raffadite, a group that believes in the superiority of The Prophet's family over his disciples.

Shafa'h, Intercession, a belief that the Messenger will intercede on the judgement day for humanity as a whole and specifically for the Muslim sinners.

Shariah, literally the path to the water hole, it refers to the Islamic laws, spiritual, morals and manners, social and economic aspects of life.

Shian-e-Ali, Shias, the friends of Ali, original name of the Shia's.

Shaykh, the venerable guide, also known as the Pir or the Murshid. Islamic scholar who was initiated in a spiritual order through all of allegiance to a established Shaykh and subsequently given permission to take oath of allegiance and carry the mantle of the Shaykh and to deputise for him.

Sunnah, the practice of the blessed Messenger, highly recommended and the habit of neglecting it is sinful.

Tasawuf, also known as Sufism, Islamic mysticism. It is the science of Islamic spirituality and the morals and the manners of the Messenger. Characterised by simple and frugal living and abundant devotional life. The Practitioner of Tasawuf is called the Sufi.

Tafdeeli, people who regard Ali superior to Abu Bakr and Umar.

Tariqah, literally the path, technically used for describing the experiential and spiritual methodologies of the Sufis.

Wajib, necessary, category of ruling that must be practised its negligence is sinful, it's but denial is not Kufr.

Zanni, presumptive something that is accepted without clear evidence and therefore is in doubtful category.

Zikr, literally the memory, Allah's remembrance, technically it's the repeated utterance of the beautiful names of Allah or significant phrases verbally and meditating over them quietly or loudly, alone or in group.